GHOSTHUNTING
SAN ANTONIO,
AUSTIN, and
TEXAS HILL COUNTRY

AMERICA'S
HAUNTED ROAD TRIP

Other Titles in the *America's Haunted Road Trip* Series:

FOLLOW US ON TWITTER: @hauntedtrips
FACEBOOK: www.facebook.com/AHRT.books
VISIT OUR WEBSITE: americashauntedroadtrip.com

GHOSTHUNTING SAN ANTONIO, AUSTIN, and TEXAS HILL COUNTRY

Michael O. Varhola

CLERISY PRESS

Ghosthunting San Antonio, Austin, and Texas Hill Country

COPYRIGHT © 2015 by Michael O. Varhola

All rights reserved. No portion of this book may be reproduced in any fashion, print, facsimile, or electronic, or by any method yet to be developed, without express permission of the copyright holder.

For further information, contact the publisher:

ℚ CLERISY PRESS
An imprint of Keen Communications, LLC
306 Greenup St.
Covington, KY 41011
clerisypress.com

Library of Congress Cataloging-in-Publication Data
Varhola, Michael O., 1966–
  Ghosthunting San Antonio, Austin, and Texas Hill Country / Michael O. Varhola. — First [edition].
      pages cm
  Includes bibliographical references.
  ISBN 978-1-57860-547-7 — ISBN 1-57860-547-4 — eISBN 978-1-57860-548-4
  1. Haunted places—Texas—San Antonio. 2. Haunted places—Texas—Austin.
  3. Haunted places—Texas—Texas Hill Country. 4. Ghosts—Texas—San Antonio.
  5. Ghosts—Texas—Austin. 6. Ghosts—Texas—Texas Hill Country. I. Title.

  BF1472.U6V365 2015
  133.109764—dc23

                              2015020430

Distributed by Publishers Group West
Printed in the United States of America
First edition, first printing

Editor: Lisa C. Bailey
Cover design: Scott McGrew
Text production: Lapiz Digital Services
Cover and interior photos: Michael O. Varhola except as noted on-page
Maps: Steve Jones
Proofreader: Rebecca Henderson

TABLE OF CONTENTS

Greater San Antonio   100

Austin   121

Texas Hill Country   153

Ghosthunting Travel Guide   183

Acknowledgments

WHILE WRITING IS A SOLITARY PURSUIT in so many ways, a striking number of people nonetheless played a role in the completion of this project and deserve recognition here.

Foremost among those who warrant thanks is my wife, Diane, who accompanied me on visits to many of the sites that appear in this book and, perhaps even more importantly, allowed me to make working on it a priority.

Three people who have encouraged the development of this project and given me an opportunity to speak about it publicly are Donna Stewart, Laura Schier, and Sharon Kincaid of Psi-Fi Radio, a paranormal-themed show I have appeared on many times over the years. All three of them even ventured out to Texas in May 2014 to do presentations and broadcast the show from the Comicpalooza fan convention in Houston!

Comicpalooza itself, for which I serve as the paranormal track coordinator, has also been a terrific venue for talking to people about haunted sites in Texas, the *America's Haunted Road Trip* series, and paranormal investigation in general. Its organizers have always been very helpful and encouraging. I am especially grateful to John and Patty Simons, Ginger Ney, and Dawn Washington.

Another convention that has given me the opportunity to talk about haunted places in the Lone Star State is Dallas Comic & Pop Expo, which is owned and operated by impresario Zachery Taylor McGinnis, with whom I always enjoy working.

I also have had the opportunity to work with a number of paranormal investigation groups while writing this book and would like to thank the members and organizers of San Antonio Ghosthunters, Dawn Paranormal, and the Pasadena Paranormal

Research Team. People in those groups whom I have particularly enjoyed working with include Jill Benoit, Christy Briones, John Delgado, Alan King, Glenn Martinez, Coy and Lori McCollum, and Kristen Stout.

Special thanks are due to Lauren Swartz and Allison Lindhorst of Sisters Grimm Ghost Tours, whose historical roots in San Antonio, paranormal research in it, and work on the subject provided me with lots of useful information and some unique perspectives.

Karen Holmes, someone whom I have worked with off and on in some capacity or other since moving to Texas in 2009, deserves thanks for encouraging me in this and other projects and discussing the history and folklore of Texas with me. She also gave me the opportunity to visit or spend time at a number of the sites described in this book, including Enchanted Rock, the Texas State Capitol, the San Antonio Missions, and the Devil's Backbone (the first three of which I visited with her and students from Fischer Schule Haus Christian Academy, and the last of which is the area where that school is located).

I do not want to neglect to thank the publishing, editorial, and design staff at Clerisy Press for the work they did on this book at their end. I am especially grateful to acquisitions editor Tim W. Jackson, who served as *de facto* project manager for this book and as my main point of contact with the company while I was working on it; to marketing and publicity specialists Liliane Opsomer and Tanya Twerdowsky Sylvan; and to publisher Richard Hunt. Molly Merkle and Marie Hillin at the Keen Communications headquarters have also always been helpful and a pleasure to work with.

A number of the proprietors or staff of various sites I visited or people I encountered in the process of doing so deserve my thanks as well, and these include Jo Ann Rivera of Victoria's Black Swan Inn, Doug Blank of the Faust Hotel, staff members at Hotel Indigo and the Emily Morgan Hotel in San Antonio and the Driskill Hotel in Austin, the staff of Ye Kendall Inn in Boerne, the management and staff of the Austin Pizza Garden, and bartender Lincoln at the Devil's Backbone Tavern.

I also would like to thank all of the editors, colleagues, family members, business associates, and friends who patiently—or, in some cases, not so patiently—waited for me to fulfill my obligations to them while I was focusing so much of my attention on this project.

Finally, if there is anyone I have left out of these acknowledgments, I would like to sincerely beg their forgiveness and thank them for the roles they played in the completion of this book as well!

Welcome to *America's Haunted Road Trip*

BY VIRTUE OF THE FACT you are reading this book, there is a pretty good chance you believe in ghosts or are at least open to the idea that something referred to as such might be real. If so, you are in pretty good company. Surveys over the years tend to show that more than half of all Americans believe in ghosts and other supernatural phenomena. Some 61% of participants in a September 2013 *Huffington Post* poll, in fact, indicated that they "believe some people have experienced ghosts." (Those overall numbers skew up by as much as 8% and down as much as 16% based on factors that include gender, age, political affiliation, race, education, and geographical region).

Paranormal phenomena that you or someone you know might have experienced can vary widely, from the subtle to the profound and the comforting to the disturbing. Many people not seeking supernatural experiences have felt the presence or touch of recently departed loved ones, for example, or even seen them, often just once, as if in final farewell. Others have at various points, and perhaps in places reputed to be haunted, experienced things like disembodied footsteps, inexplicable cold spots, or sounds with no discernible sources, including someone calling their names.

Those who are psychically sensitive, exposed to extremely haunted sites, or actively engage in paranormal investigations of various sorts, of course—including what have been widely referred to for some years now as ghost hunts—might experience any number of other things as well. These can include anomalies not audible to the naked ear or visible to the naked eye captured in recordings or photographs, such as electronic voice phenomena (EVPs) in the former and orbs, mists, or even coveted full-frontal apparitions in the latter.

Our intent with the *America's Haunted Road Trip* series is to provide readers with resources they can use to personally discover and explore publicly accessible places that might be occupied by ghosts or the sites of other paranormal activity. We are not in the business of trying to prove that any particular place is or is not haunted; every single one of the places that appears in *Ghosthunting San Antonio, Austin, and Texas Hill Country* certainly could be, and I firmly believe that a number of them definitely are. The purpose of this volume and the others in the series is to tell everyone, from the casual historical traveler to the hard-core ghosthunter, about places of potential interest to them and to provide actionable, concrete information about how to visit those places.

As noted, all of the places covered in this book and the other volumes of the *America's Haunted Road Trip* series are, to a lesser or greater extent, publicly accessible; there is simply no point in creating a travel guide to places people cannot easily visit. Sorts of places we cover in our guidebooks therefore include appropriate bridges, cemeteries and graveyards, churches and other places of worship, colleges and universities, government buildings, historic sites, hotels, museums, neighborhoods/districts of towns or cities, parks, railroads, restaurants and bars, roads and highways, shopping areas and malls, sports stadiums, and theaters.

Sorts of places we do not cover in our guidebooks or encourage people to visit generally include assisted-living facilities; elementary, middle, or high schools; hospitals; private homes and residential apartment buildings; private property; or prohibited areas like abandoned mental institutions or condemned buildings. It also bears mentioning that all potentially haunted places, their intersection with the other world notwithstanding, are still subject to all the hazards of the real world. So, show due respect to other good people and watch out for bad ones, do not fall afoul of local laws, be prepared for environmental hazards, and, in keeping with the mantra of respectful exploration, "take nothing but photographs, leave nothing but footprints."

Beyond that, we hope this book and the others in the series will be useful to you and that you have an enjoyable, informative, and fulfilling journey on your own haunted road trip!

—*Michael O. Varhola*
Editor, America's Haunted Road Trip
varhola@varhola.com

INTRODUCTION

TO SAY THAT I LIVE IN THE MIDST of a haunted landscape would hardly be an exaggeration. About a half mile east of my home, in the little wooded valley below the ridge it sits on, lies a tiny, haunted, 19th-century German graveyard, its half-dozen headstones clustered around an ancient oak and enclosed in a rickety fence. A half mile west of my home, the deep, overgrown ravine known as Devil's Hollow—a dry creek bed within which ancient peoples once lived—descends from the spine of low, rocky mountains to the north. Four miles north of my home, the haunted highway that locals call the Devil's Backbone runs along the top of the aforementioned chain. And, on a miniature charter-school campus located on that road, between a haunted one-room schoolhouse and a somewhat desolate historic cemetery, I have taught children history.

Innumerable haunted and otherwise strange or spiritually charged sites of every sort radiate out from there in every direction, as if from the center of a supernatural vortex. Forty miles south, in the heart of San Antonio, you will find some of the most haunted locales in all of Texas, including the Alamo and the hotels that sit on the site of the battle that was fought around it, the Crockett and the Menger. Within blocks of these two are other hotels, colonial Spanish buildings, and the oldest continuously used cathedral in North America, all haunted by the ghosts of people who dwelled, visited, or worked in them in life. A little farther away lie the Ghost Tracks, where spectral children are known to move people's stopped cars. If you head 25 miles east, you will come to the town of New Braunfels, which houses the historic village of Gruene and the beautiful and creepy Faust Hotel. Fifty miles north, in the state capital of Austin, government buildings remain occupied by the spirits of officials, their mistresses, and others who met strange or violent ends there, and numerous haunted parks, restaurants, and other sites can be found. And for a hundred miles north and west, up into the rugged, rolling highlands known as Hill Country, uncounted haunted crossroads, caves, wilderness areas, and towns dot the landscape.

Urban legends abound in the area about things like zombie outbreaks and supposed encounters with devils at dance halls, as well as accounts of cryptozoological creatures like the Donkey Lady and *chupacabra,* UFOs and alien encounters, and other paranormal but nonghostly phenomena. We have decided that these things stray too far from the core subject of this book, however, and that they do not quite fit in with places reputed to be haunted by ghosts. Maybe one day they will warrant a book of their own!

Texas is certainly one of the most haunted of all the states, as befits its vast size; long, violent history; and brief status as an independent nation. And, settled by Spanish explorers more than three centuries ago, San Antonio in particular has a rich haunted history that includes conquistadores, the local Apache and Comanche Indian tribes, old monasteries, lost gold mines, battlefields, and elegant hotels. Perhaps because of its blood-stained heritage, people have also always felt the presence of evil and the supernatural in Texas, evidence of which remains in the names of desolate, isolated, or forbidding places throughout the state—names like the Devil's River, Devil's Sinkhole, and Purgatory Road. Perhaps the iniquity that has occurred in Texas has inspired people to see the devil in its landscape, or perhaps he really is present and has inspired much of the evil that has been perpetrated here and the spiritual residua that remains.

My own interest in the paranormal goes back as long as I can remember, in large part from having spent the first half of my life visiting spiritually charged or haunted places like the Tower of London in England, the Parthenon in Athens, the Paris Catacombs, old Nazi tunnels in Germany, and scores of castles throughout Europe. My attraction to the strange history of the American Southwest goes back just as far and is rooted in experiences that include family trips into the California desert, a year living on an Indian reservation in Roswell, New Mexico, and pilgrimages to ancient Spanish churches in Colorado.

Since childhood I have also loved the classic song "Ghost Riders in the Sky," a cowboy-style ballad that dates to 1948 and has been recorded by more than 50 performers. Unmatched in poignantly evoking the haunted tradition of Texas and the Southwest, it tells the tale of a cowboy who encounters a herd of spectral cattle being chased eternally across the sky by the damned spirits of cowboys. Hearing it never fails to raise the hair on the back of my neck:

An old cowboy went ridin' out one dark and windy day
Upon a ridge he rested as he went along his way
When all at once a mighty herd of red-eyed cows he saw
Plowin' through the ragged skies, and up a cloudy draw

Their brands were still on fire and their hooves were made
    of steel
Their horns were black and shiny and their hot breath he
    could feel
A bolt of fear went through him as they thundered through
    the sky
For he saw the riders comin' hard, and he heard their mournful
    cries

Yippie i ohhh ohh ohh
Yippie i aye ye ye
Ghost riders in the sky
Their faces gaunt, their eyes were blurred
Their shirts all soaked with sweat

He's ridin' hard to catch that herd
But he ain't caught 'em yet
Cause they got to ride forever in that range up in the sky
On horses snortin' fire, as they ride on hear their cries

As the riders loped on by him he heard one call his name
If you wanna save your soul from hell a-ridin' on our range
Then cowboy change your ways today or with us you will ride
Tryin' to catch the devil's herd, across these endless skies

Yippie i ohhh oh oh
Yippie i aye ye ye
Ghost riders in the sky
Ghost riders in the sky
Ghost riders in the sky

I have drawn upon these experiences, as well as my training and background as a historian, journalist, and paranormal investigator, in compiling what I hope is a colorful and useful guide to publicly accessible haunted places. My intent is for it to appeal both to residents of and visitors to one of the largest and fastest-growing metropolitan areas in the United States, especially those interested in the paranormal, travel, or Texas history.

Ghosthunting San Antonio, Austin, and Texas Hill Country covers nearly three dozen haunted locations in or around the cities of San Antonio and Austin and throughout Texas Hill Country, collectively one of the most haunted places in the country. Each chapter includes a combination of history, haunted lore and phenomena, and practical visitation information. This hands-on guide is organized into four geographical sections—San Antonio, Greater San Antonio, Austin, and Texas Hill Country—and includes all the information readers will need to visit the places described in it. This book also includes an appendix that briefly

describes nearly 100 other haunted places in the region that people can go to, making it even more comprehensive.

All of the places described in this book are believed to be haunted. That said, determining exactly what ghosts are is beyond the scope of this book, and throughout it I use terms like *ghost*, *phantasm*, *specter*, and *spirit* fairly synonymously and not as technical terms indicating manifestations with specific and differing characteristics. This is, after all, primarily a travel guide, not a tome devoted to the classification of earthbound spirits, which would be of little practical use to most readers. All that said, the term *ghosts* runs the gamut from nonsentient residues of spiritual energy that can be detected by various means, to intelligent manifestations that can make their presence felt in various ways. My sense is that the vast majority of hauntings are of the lower order and that it is quite possible to have subtly haunted sites that are never identified as such due to a lack of investigation.

My goal with this book is not to prove that any of the places included in it are indeed haunted, just to identify sites that have ghostly phenomena associated with them, to visit them, and to compile their histories and my experiences into a book that other people with an interest in the subject can use as a guide for their own visits. That said, I am willing to go on the record and say that I believe any of the sites covered in this book *could* be haunted—and I am firmly convinced that several of them definitely are. I will leave to readers to determine for themselves which ones those might be.

Ghosthunting as a pursuit has certainly come into its own over the past several years, and it and associated phenomena have become the subjects of numerous television shows and movies. In my experience, however, actual paranormal investigation bears very little resemblance to what is depicted even in "reality" shows related to the subject. The real thing is generally much less manic, a lot quieter, and—despite the absence of noise, running back and forth, and jerky camera angles—much more intense. It also does not result in evidence of paranormal activity on every expedition.

Many paranormal investigators today use a wide variety of electronic equipment, and there can certainly be some value associated with this approach. I do not believe, however, anyone should hesitate to engage in ghosthunting based on a lack of equipment, and am myself more of a "naturalistic" ghosthunter. For various reasons, I use a minimum of equipment in my own investigations and not much more than I have ever used as a writer and reporter: a digital recorder, a digital camera, a pen and notepad, and a flashlight. I also have found a full tank of gas, some food and water, and a fully charged cell phone to be useful when heading into relatively isolated areas.

I also think a ghosthunter's innate senses are just as critical to an investigation as any sort of equipment. While I make no claims here to be psychic or a medium, I do believe that most people have access to certain paranormal senses that they can draw upon if they choose to and are aware of them. People who can use such abilities reliably have generally spent many years honing them and learning to differentiate exterior phenomena from internal thoughts. Those without such experience should probably err on the side of caution and, in the absence of corroborating evidence, assume that whatever they are sensing could very well be a product of their imaginations.

Beyond experience, a good attitude is crucial. While the following chapters include a lot of information that can be useful when visiting the specific sites, there is one bit of general advice I would like offer to prospective ghosthunters: Show respect for both the rights of any relevant living people (for example, property owners) and for the dignity of any spirits that might be lingering at a particular site. I believe that paranormal investigation is an endeavor fraught with its own potential hazards, and my sense is that anyone who acts inappropriately for too long is ultimately going to suffer some unhappy consequences—whether legal, spiritual, or otherwise.

The point of this book is not for me to convince anybody of anything. Rather, it is to provide a tool that historic travelers and prospective ghosthunters can use to help them find haunted sites, conduct their own investigations, and draw their own conclusions. I sincerely hope you enjoy this book and find it to be a useful resource on your own haunted road trip through San Antonio, Austin, and Texas Hill Country!

—*Michael O. Varhola*
Canyon Lake, Texas

San Antonio

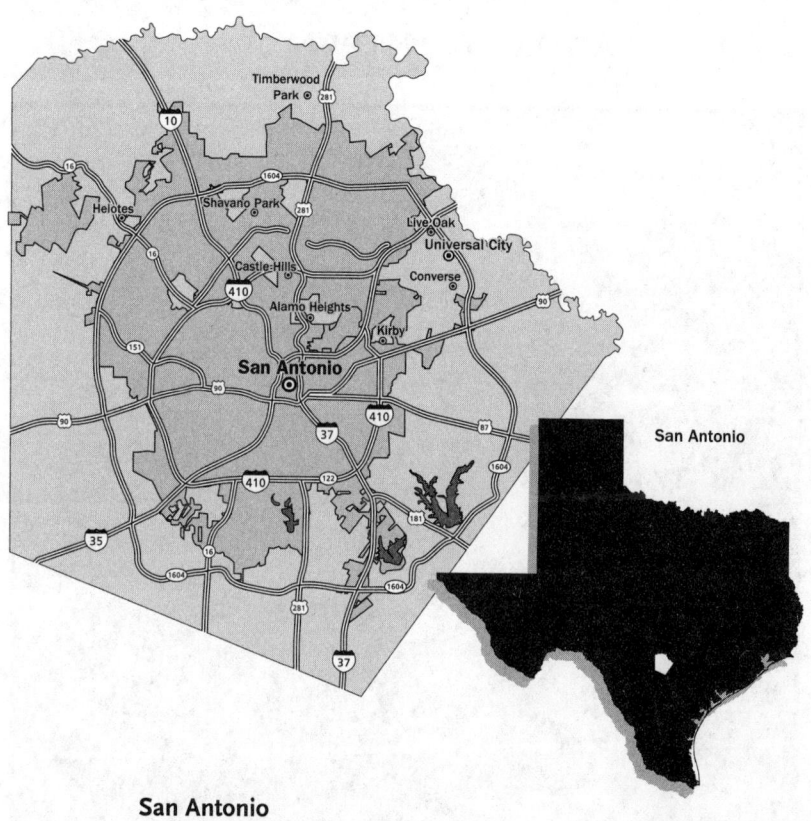

San Antonio

San Antonio
 San Antonio Missions
 Alamodome
 Alamo Quarry Market
 Comanche Lookout Park
 Crockett Hotel
 Emily Morgan Hotel
 Menger Hotel
 Old Bexar County Jail
 San Fernando Cathedral
 Sheraton Gunter Hotel San Antonio
 Spanish Governor's Palace
 University of the Incarnate Word
 Victoria's Black Swan Inn

CHAPTER 1

San Antonio Missions
SOUTH AND DOWNTOWN SAN ANTONIO

WHILE THE ALAMO is certainly the most famous site in Texas, it is amazing how many people do not know that it was originally just one of several Spanish missions established along the banks of the San Antonio River. Originally called Mission San Antonio de Valero, it was the first and northernmost of six religious settlements defended by the garrison from the presidio of San Antonio de Bexar. Over the next 13 years, four other significant church communities were established: Mission San José, Mission Espada, Mission San Juan, Mission Najera, and Mission Concepción.

All of these missions were part of a broader colonial network of frontier outposts established by Roman Catholic religious orders that stretched across the Southwest from the 1600s through the 1800s. Their main purpose was to facilitate conversion of local Indian populations and to reinforce New Spain against incursions by France. A number of the San Antonio missions had originally been established in other places a decade or two earlier, but after they failed—in part because of ambivalence or even hostility from the native peoples to whom they were trying to minister—they were relocated.

"A Spanish mission was much more than a religious institution," the Alamo says in its official history. "Its purpose was to take an indigenous population and convert them not only to Catholicism but also to the Spanish way of life. In establishing the missions in Texas, the Spanish hoped to create a self-sufficient population that would continue to exist and grow as loyal Spanish subjects, thereby staving off any involvement of foreign powers like France. Indian converts were taught farming, livestock raising, blacksmithing, carpentry, stone work, and weaving."

Missionaries and Indians alike also found protection and the means of defending themselves at the missions. But, while the missions themselves were virtual fortresses, men working in the fields and livestock were vulnerable.

"Encroachment by warlike Apaches from the west and Comanches from the north meant local Coahuiltecan tribes were under constant threat," the history continues. "Mission life brought protection from other indigenous people as well as shelter and a more stable food supply. It also gave them access to two important technological developments of the period: firearms and horses."

Over all, building, maintaining, and running the settlements and the infrastructure associated with them proved an impressive architectural and logistical feat. One aspect of this was the construction of *acequias,* water management systems originally introduced into arid regions of Spain by the Romans and Moors and which were carried into the deserts of the New World by the Franciscan missionaries. In order to distribute water to their missions along the San Antonio River, they oversaw construction of a network of gravity-flow ditches, dams, and at least one aqueduct, comprising a 15-mile system used to irrigate some 3,500 acres of land.

By the end of the 18th century, the Indian populations had greatly diminished on the missions for a combination of reasons, including discontent and mortality caused by European diseases to which the natives had little resistance. This reduced the viability and need for the missions, so, with more settlers moving into the area and looking covetously at the holdings of the religious communities, government authorities forced them to divest most of their assets. In 1793–94, all of the San Antonio missions were secularized and their lands and other property turned over to the families still residing on them or to Spanish locals. Some of the churches continued to remain active after this point, but others were closed and many of the missions fell into disrepair or were largely abandoned.

Over their centuries of existence, what are now collectively known as the San Antonio missions were the starting points of quests north and west in search of gold and souls, locations of raids and battles, places of births and deaths. They were crucibles of human emotion—those of fervent proselytes spreading the word of God, native peoples being stripped of their own cultures and faiths, greedy and bloodthirsty fortune hunters, and those who fell in battle at their gates or succumbed to disease within their walls. All were also established in an abundant area that had been occupied by ancient peoples since time immemorial and used by them for hunting and gathering. It should thus not be surprising that these missions are widely considered to be haunted and that people have reported every sort of paranormal phenomena at them, including anomalies in photographs and recordings and apparitions of conquistadores, monks, Indians, settlers, and soldiers.

Mission San Antonio de Valero (a.k.a. the Alamo)

In 1718, after Mission San Francisco de Solano in the Rio Grande Valley became unviable because so many of its resident Coahuiltecan Indians had left it, Father Antonio de San Buenaventura y Olivares relocated it to a spot near the headwaters of the San Antonio River. He had passed through the area a decade earlier and been impressed with its suitability for a religious community. He named the new mission in honor of Saint Anthony of Padua and San Antonio de Valero, the Spanish viceroy who had approved his plan.

Location of the mission changed several times for the first few years until 1724, when the present site was chosen, and the foundation of its stone church was laid 20 years later, in 1744. It eventually included a walled compound containing the church, a *convento* where the clergymen lived, and a number of adobe buildings.

While the Alamo is almost synonymous with the battle that bears its name, it was by no means the first time the mission or its residents were exposed to violence or dangers. On June 30, 1745, for example, Apaches attacked the nearby civil town of San Fernando. One hundred mission converts from the Alamo sallied out and, reinforced by European arms and tactics, helped drive them off.

Mission San Antonio de Valero was the first of the local missions to be secularized and was taken over by Spanish authorities in 1793. They established the first hospital in Texas in it. Its central location and infrastructure also made it ideal for use as a barracks and, by 1803, a company of 100 heavily armed cavalrymen, along with their families, had moved into it. They remained there for 32 years, battling Indians, the military adventurers known as filibusters, and revolutionaries. When Mexico became independent of Spain in 1821, they shifted their allegiance to the new nation. And when they skirmished with Anglo-American revolutionaries near the town of Gonzales on October 2, 1835, the Texas Revolution began.

Texian forces counterattacked toward the end of that month and laid siege to San Antonio. Then, on December 5, they attacked the town directly and, after fighting the Mexican troops toe-to-toe in brutal street fighting for five days, forced the military authorities to surrender. Thus it was that the Texians took control of the city. When General Antonio López de Santa Anna arrived at the head of a Mexican army on February 23, 1836, the Texians withdrew to the east bank of the San Antonio River and occupied the Alamo. Santa Anna raised the red flag of no quarter over San Fernando church, and a siege of the mission began.

On March 6, Santa Anna launched his final attack on the Alamo and, after a fierce 90-minute battle, captured it and slew all 189 of its defenders, at a cost of about 600 killed and wounded among his own men. Commanders William Barret

Travis, James Bowie, and David Crockett were among those who fell in battle. Santa Anna ordered all the bodies burned on at least two common pyres and left to smolder for days (although that of one defender, Tejano Gregorio Esparza, whose brother was one of the Mexican officers, received a proper burial).

Six weeks later, on April 21, Texian forces led by Sam Houston defeated Santa Anna and the Mexican army in the Battle of San Jacinto, about 200 miles to the east. The following month, the Mexican garrison in San Antonio was ordered to destroy the Alamo and then withdraw. They did manage to tear down some of the outer walls, and their commander, Juan José Andrade, sent a detachment of men to blow up the church where the defenders had made their final stand. These men were reportedly prevented from doing so, however, by a party of what they identified as *diablos*. They were described by paranormal researcher Docia Schultz Williams in her book *Spirits of San Antonio and South*

Texas as "six ghostly forms standing in a semicircle holding swords, not of steel but of fire, blocking their entry to the building."

"They were terrified and fearful of the consequences if they should destroy the building, they reported back to their commander," Williams continues. "It is said General Andrade went himself to the place and was also confronted by the same figures. And so it was that the building was left intact as the Mexican army marched out of San Antonio."

Apparitions were reported again at the site in 1871—which at that point was being used as a police station—when the city tore down part of the surviving mission complex, a pair of rooms that had been located to either side of the main gate in the south wall. Guests at the Menger Hotel across the street were among those who claimed to see spectral soldiers marching along the perimeter of the old mission compound as if trying to defend it from further desecration.

Many people, too, have striven to protect the legacy of the Alamo. In the 1930s, as the centennial of the Battle of the Alamo approached, the entire complex was renovated, expanded, and converted into a parklike memorial, and a Centennial Museum was built behind the church (and currently serves as the gift shop for the site). Then, in 1968, the Daughters of the Republic of Texas opened a new museum in the *convento,* or "long barrack," finally putting the oldest building on the mission grounds back into use.

MISSION SAN JOSÉ

MISSION SAN JOSÉ Y SAN MIGUEL DE AGUAYO, more commonly known simply as Mission San José, was founded on February 23, 1720, because Mission San Antonio de Valero (the Alamo) had, soon after its establishment, become overcrowded with refugees from missions shut down in East

Texas. Franciscan priest Antonio Margil received permission from the Marquis de San Miguel de Aguayo, the governor of Coahuila y Texas, to build a new mission 5 miles south of the presidio of San Antonio de Bexar. Like a number of other missions in the area, it ministered to the local Coahuiltecan Indians.

Initially made of brush, straw, and mud, Mission San José's first buildings were soon replaced by large stone structures that included offices, a dining room, a pantry, and guest rooms. The main portion of the compound was enclosed in a thick outer wall that had built into it rooms for 350 native residents. Its impressive limestone church—which stands to this day and was distinguished by a dome, two towers, and an elaborately carved facade—was completed in 1768. The remarkable complex reached its full extent by 1782. It was the largest and most elaborate of the San Antonio religious communities, dubbed "Queen of the Missions."

"It is, in truth, the first mission in America," friar Juan Agustín Morfí wrote in his journal. "In point of beauty, plan, and strength . . . there is not a presidio along the entire frontier line that can compare with it." Two soldiers from the nearby presidio of San Antonio de Bexar helped provide security for the complex and trained its residents in the use of firearms and artillery.

Like the other local missions, Mission San José turned over its lands to its resident Indians in 1794, and religious activities at the site were officially ended in 1824. In the years that followed, the mission fell into disrepair and its buildings were variously abandoned or occupied by soldiers, vagabonds, and bandits. It was restored in the 1920s and 1930s, much of it by the federal government's Works Progress Administration; declared a State Historical Site in 1941; and added to the National Register of Historic Places in 1978.

On the night of July 31–August 1, 2000, thieves stole three Spanish Colonial–era statues that sat at the altar of the church at Mission San José. These painted, carved wooden statues, each of which stood 3 and 4 feet in height, are considered priceless because of their age and profound historical and religious significance, but their fate remains unknown.

MISSION ESPADA

MISSION ESPADA WAS ESTABLISHED on a spot near the San Antonio River in 1731, having been moved from its original location in what is now Augusta, Texas—about 150 miles north of present-day Houston—where it had enjoyed a tumultuous and bloody history since 1690. Its Franciscan founders built a friary in 1745 and completed the church in 1756.

Missionaries at the site converted the resident Coahuiltecan Indians to Christianity and instructed them in the principles of

architecture and masonry, blacksmithing, brick and tile making, farming and ranching, and spinning and weaving.

By the time secularization of the San Antonio missions began
in 1794, Mission Espada was impoverished, had declined badly,
and had just 15 families still associated with it, each of which was
granted a parcel of land. It functioned communally for a time, with
the residents sharing supplies and equipment. Misfortune befell
the community in 1826, first when a band of Comanches raided
the cornfields and slaughtered all the livestock, and later when a
kitchen fire destroyed most of its buildings.

During the period 1858–1907, a Claretian priest named
Francis Bouchu resided at the mission and restored many of the
collapsing buildings inside the compound, but progress slowed
when he departed and the church was temporarily closed for
repairs. It was reopened in 1915 by priests from the Diocese of
San Antonio, and a school was established inside the compound
by nuns from the Order of the Incarnate Word and Blessed Sacrament. They ran the school for more than five decades until
1967, when it was shut down and the Franciscans once again
took charge of Mission Espada.

Today, visitors to the mission can see the best-preserved
example of a historic Spanish Colonial *acequia,* which includes
the still-working Espada aqueduct and dam. Its main ditch continues to carry water to the mission and its former farmlands
and is still used by residents of the local area.

Mission San Juan

Originally founded in 1716 as La Misión San
José de los Nazonis in East Texas, Mission San Juan Capistrano also was established by Spanish Franciscans on the eastern banks of the San Antonio River in 1731. It was named for

Saint John of Capistrano, a 15th-century theologian and warrior priest who resided in the Abruzzo region of Italy.

The missionaries constructed San Juan's first chapel from mud and brush and eventually added to it a tower containing two bells. Then, around 1756, they replaced this primitive building with a long hall with a flat roof and a more substantial belfry that remains on the site to this day. They also constructed a dam in order to provide water for the mission's *acequia* irrigation system.

"San Juan was a self-sustaining community. Within the compound, Indian artisans produced iron tools, cloth, and prepared hides," Kathy Weiser writes in her *Legends of America* online magazine. "Orchards and gardens outside the walls provided melons, pumpkins, grapes, and peppers. Beyond the mission complex, Indian farmers cultivated corn, beans, squash, sweet potatoes, and sugar cane in irrigated fields . . . . By the mid-1700s, San Juan, with its rich farm and pasturelands, was a regional supplier of agricultural produce. With its surplus, San Juan established a trade network stretching east to Louisiana and south to Coahuila, Mexico. This thriving economy helped the mission to survive epidemics and Indian attacks in its final years."

Despite its prosperity, however, Mission San Juan was not able to maintain a large native population, and that affected its viability. At its height in 1756, for example, some 265 Coahuiltecan Indian neophytes lived at the mission, but 34 years later only 58 lived there. It was then that the missionaries broke ground on a larger church building on the east side of the complex, but they were never able to complete it. Work on it was abandoned and, eventually, it was used as a crypt for native residents.

Mission San Juan was secularized in 1794 and had a decreasing level of religious activity until 1824, when it ended altogether. The site was largely abandoned until 1840, when priests from the Diocese of San Antonio resumed conducting mass at it.

In 1934, some of the Indian quarters and the foundations of the unfinished church were unearthed as part of a public works project. Then, in the 1960s, the chapel, priests' quarters, and other structures were reconstructed. Today most of the original plaza remains within the courtyard walls and authentically depicts the floor plan and layout. Members of the Claretian and Redemptorist orders also held services at the site until 1967, when the Franciscans once again took control of the mission.

MISSION CONCEPCIÓN

FRANCISCAN FRIARS ESTABLISHED Misión Nuestra
Señora de la Purísima Concepción de Acuña, more commonly
referred to simply as Mission Concepción, near the San Antonio River in 1731. Most of the native people in the mission
were Pajalats, a local tribe that used to live in the area south
of San Antonio, and their chiefs served as governors of the
affiliated Indian community.

At least one large battle took place between Spanish settlers
and Indians here, resulting in great loss of life, in the 1700s.
Then, on October 28, 1835, the first significant battle of the Texas
Revolution was fought between Texian insurgents, led by James
Bowie and James Fannin, and Mexican soldiers under the command of Colonel Domingo Ugartechea. About 90 of the Texians
had encamped near the mission while searching for a suitable and
relatively safe place for the remainder of the army to rest when

they were attacked by a mixed force of about 275 Mexican infantry, cavalry, and artillery. The Texians took cover in a U-shaped gully and, between their defensive position and superior small arms, drove off the Mexican troops in the ensuing 30-minute battle, winning the Battle of Concepción. One Texian and as many as 76 Mexican troops were slain during the skirmish.

On October 31, 1984, the *San Antonio Express-News* ran a story that described activity experienced in the area around Mission Concepción and some of the possible reasons for it. "Some 300 soldiers died in that area during an 18th-century battle near the mission. A Dr. Navarro, who lived there around the turn of the century, is said to have murdered Juana, who was either his live-in maid or his lover. Nobody knows for sure," this account reads. It goes on to describe how, while saying a rosary, a local resident "saw a plume of smoke waft in from a back room. Forming a column in front of him, it didn't take on masculine or feminine features . . . but simply stood and watched him. He moved towards the apparition and it disappeared. Going back to his rosary, the column of smoke reappeared."

Mission Concepción is the best preserved of the Texas missions, remains active as a church with a congregation that attends Sunday mass there to this day, and in 2009–2010 had its interior completely restored.

With their strange, turbulent, and violent histories, and events that have included abandonment, violence, death, fervent passions, theft of holy relics, and the full range of human emotions, it is not surprising that the San Antonio missions would be haunted. People have reported paranormal phenomena of all sorts at them, including relatively prosaic things like inexplicable cold spots and a feeling of melancholy on the one hand, to full-blown apparitions on the other, and everything from anomalies like EVPs to orbs in between. There are perhaps no better places to get a sense for the history of San Antonio, mundane and paranormal alike.

CHAPTER 2

Alamodome
Downtown San Antonio

Wikimedia Commons/Billy Hathorn

WHEN ONE CONSIDERS what sorts of places are most likely to be haunted, they might not necessarily think of large, public, relatively new structures like event arenas constructed during the past two or three decades. But almost everything is built where other things with their own histories used to be and on ground that may have already been a site of spiritual activity. And even places that are the brightest under the best of conditions sometimes have dark pasts of their own. Short of a battlefield, there are perhaps few places where so many people congregate in one place and express such strong emotions as a sports stadium. It should thus not be too surprising that people have, over the years, reported so much paranormal activity at the Alamodome.

Located at the southeastern edge of downtown San Antonio, the Alamodome is a domed, five-level, multipurpose, rectilinear venue that has been used for everything from basketball and football games to musical concerts to conventions and trade shows. It was designed so that it could easily be converted into a basketball or hockey arena, and, in this configuration, it can seat 20,662 spectators if only the two lower levels are used, and up to 39,500 if seats in the upper level are also opened. It can seat up to 65,000 spectators for a typical football game but be expanded to accommodate a full 72,000, meaning it is able to host a Super Bowl game if that opportunity should arise.

"The Alamodome is what is known as a 'third-generation' facility," according to its official history. "It features column-free spans for unobstructed viewing and curtain wall system for configuration flexibility. [It has] the advantage of both a convention center and a dome without the drawbacks of either [and] is large enough to easily accommodate assemblies and trade shows. The column-free design makes it unlike other domes in one very important way: It has an intimate, 'human' scale."

This $186 million brick, concrete, steel, and glass facility, owned and operated by the city of San Antonio, opened to the public on May 15, 1993. Among other things, it was intended to increase the city's convention traffic, attract a professional football franchise, qualify the city to host the Olympic Games, and placate demands by the San Antonio Spurs basketball team for a larger arena.

The city did briefly have a professional World League of American Football team, the San Antonio Riders, in 1991–92, but after the organization withdrew from North America, the team collapsed and never had a chance to play in the new stadium. And, for better or worse, San Antonio has not been able to attract an NFL team. The Spurs, however, did actually play in the Alamodome for a decade, 1993–2002, but became disenchanted with it and cajoled Bexar County into constructing a new arena for them, now known as the AT&T Center and their current home. The Alamodome also has hosted many trade shows and events that include Monster Jam, Disney on Ice, and the annual Valero Alamo Bowl. Country music singer George Strait performed at the Alamodome in June of 2013 and set an all-time record for the largest concert ever played in San Antonio, with some 73,086 people in attendance.

Living beings are apparently not the only ones drawn to the Alamodome, and in the years since it opened, many spirits and episodes of supernatural activity have been reported there. A variety of factors may have contributed to this. These include skirmishes fought on this ground in the early years of the city's history, it previously being the site of a blighted neighborhood where many people had been victimized over the years, and a number of people being killed in the Alamodome itself. Such back stories range from what sound very much like fairly universal urban legends to verifiable incidents of terrible and, in some cases, hideous deaths.

Paranormal phenomena people claim to have experienced at the stadium include inexplicable cold spots, the smell of lilacs, and the feeling of a presence in a particular section of the stadium seating; doors opening on their own and lights turning themselves on and off throughout the complex; loud pounding on one of the upper-floor windows; evidence of the presence of specific ghosts; and sightings of numerous apparitions.

In one such episode, a maintenance crew that was cleaning the windows on the ground floor reportedly saw the apparition of a distressed woman dressed in 19th-century frontier garb float toward the exterior of the front door and begin knocking on it. Other people claim to have seen the specter of a

Wikimedia Commons/Greverod

lost-looking woman wandering around the parking lot, and she has been associated with a woman who is believed to have been raped and murdered at the site years before the stadium was built. Another episode involves a construction worker who was reportedly walking on a high beam while the Alamodome was being built who misstepped and plunged to his death. People have reportedly seen his ghost gliding through the long halls of the stadium.

"When I worked at the Alamodome . . . there were always strange things going on," a former employee of the venue told John Delgado of San Antonio Ghost Hunters. "A man died in the elevator shaft and that same elevator would show floor numbers on its digital readout that the dome didn't have!" She also mentioned an escalator that would stop and start on its own.

One of the verifiable and especially horrible deaths that occurred at the Alamodome also has been associated with paranormal phenomena, including footsteps, moaning, mumbling, and shadowy apparitions.

"A stunt driver was killed Saturday night when the top of his car was sheared off during a planned midair collision gone awry," the Associated Press reported on November 15, 1993. "His wife and 3-year-old son watched from the audience. Randy Hill, 49, of Phoenix died instantly when his car was struck by another car driven by daredevil Spanky Spangler, who was not injured, organizers said. Hill retired from stunt driving eight years ago and only recently decided to do the stunt at the two-day San Antonio Thrill Show at the Alamodome. The two cars were supposed to meet head-on at 50 miles per hour. Organizers did not immediately know what went wrong. The rest of the show was canceled after the accident."

The hapless Hill's tragic death is not the only one at the Alamodome associated with ghostly activity. "On September 21, 2006, around 5 p.m., a roof collapsed and trapped two employees under the rubble," attorney Beth Janicek wrote for *The Legal Examiner.* "The men were working on a structure for the Builders Showcase Expo that [was] set to open September 28, 2006. Most of the workers had finished for the day and only the two men were left on the structure." Twenty-year-old Andres Duran was killed by falling pieces of timber and tile, and some people believe that his unquiet spirit is among those that continue to haunt the massive entertainment venue.

Not a week goes by where something is not happening at the Alamodome, and very few of the hundreds of thousands of people who attend events at it each year will experience anything of a paranormal nature. Even those who do might not realize it or acknowledge that they have. But if you go to the stadium, be sure to enjoy the game, or concert, trade show, or whatever else has brought you there—and stay alert for whatever unofficial but very real paranormal events might be going on around you.

CHAPTER 3

Alamo Quarry Market
NORTH CENTRAL SAN ANTONIO

ADMITTEDLY, I tend to be more than usually skeptical when I hear reports about shopping centers and the like being haunted and to give a hard look at whether there is, in fact, a credible reason why they would be. In the case of the Alamo Quarry Market, however, it does not take too much digging to reveal that, being located just a few miles from the headwaters of the San Antonio River, it has been continuously inhabited since time immemorial. More than 10,000 years ago, Paleo-Indians hunted and gathered throughout the abundant area, and every group of people who have followed them, from Apaches and Comanches to

Spaniards, Mexicans, and Anglo-Americans, have availed themselves of its riches as well. Prior to being adapted for commercial use, in fact, it was the site of the sprawling Alamo Cement
Company factory, and many elements of the old industrial complex have been retained and even incorporated into the shopping
center. So, Alamo Quarry Market has more than enough history
behind it to make a case for it being haunted.

In the late 19th century, Englishman William Loyd discovered what he believed to be a natural cement rock in what is now
nearby Brackenridge Park and had chemist George H. Kalteyer
confirm that its lime and clay could produce what is known as
Portland cement. Loyd proceeded to organize a group of investors to form the Alamo Portland and Roman Cement Company
in 1880 (a name shortened the following year to simply Alamo
Cement Company). It was the first such cement plant west of the
Mississippi and one of the earliest in the United States. Initially
powered by steam engine, it ground 10 barrels of cement a day.

Alamo Cement Company quickly expanded and diversified
its operations, burning lime, selling building stone, constructing sidewalks, and even obtaining from the original inventor the
patent rights for segmented sidewalks that could better accommodate expansion and contraction caused by seasonal temperature changes. Its main product however, was Alamo-brand
cement, which was used widely in building projects, large and
small, throughout Texas, including the state capitol building
and the Driskill Hotel, both in Austin.

After Kalteyer died in 1897, Charles Baumberger became
president of the company and set about further expanding it. In
1908, it was reorganized under the name San Antonio Portland
Cement Company. Eventually the cement material at the Brackenridge location was exhausted. The site was then abandoned
and the plant relocated to an area some distance away that came
to be known as "Cementville." The original site became known

as Baumberger Plaza in 1944 and was eventually placed on the National Register of Historic Places, while the quarry itself became the Japanese sunken gardens at Brackenridge Park.

Alamo Quarry Market, a snazzy outdoor shopping plaza dubbed a "lifestyle center" by its developers, is located in San Antonio's Lincoln Heights neighborhood and near its Alamo Heights and Terrell Hills areas. It incorporates many elements from the old cement factory into its architecture, including the original kiln. Its stores include Ann Taylor, Coldwater Creek, Old Navy, Nordstrom Rack, Office Max, Pottery Barn, Whole Foods Market, Michael's, and Tous among others. Dining options are provided by California Pizza Kitchen, Chili's, J. Alexander's, Joe's Crab Shack, Orange Cup, PF Chang's, Piatti, and Starbuck's. What catches people's eyes from miles away and can be seen most clearly from nearby Highway 281, however, are the five huge cement factory smokestacks.

These immense structures are 36 feet wide at their bases and 30 feet wide at their tops and soar more than 200 feet above the shopping area. They were previously retrofitted with steel bands every 20 feet from top to bottom, but these components had either rusted and fallen off or become loosened, providing little if any structural reinforcement. In 1998, the owner of the property responded to this by bringing in structural restoration and preservation specialist Delta Structural Technology Inc. to restore and preserve three of the smokestacks. That company utilized an exclusive retrofit technique that involved complete encapsulation of the smokestacks using high-performance structural composites saturated in an epoxy matrix. This process took about two months and was recognized with multiple awards from the historical preservation community and concrete construction industry.

One of the most haunted parts of the shopping area is reputed to be the Regal Alamo Quarry Stadium 16-movie theater, the largest establishment in the retail complex and one that actually incorporates old plant machinery into its decor. According to local legends, bodies were entombed in its foundations when it was being built and, while details on this atrocity are somewhat vague, some people claim that the spirits of these unfortunates now haunt the site. Reported paranormal activity there includes feeling inexplicable cold spots throughout the second floor of the theater, lights in the auditorium slowly dimming and then coming fully on and then repeating the process, and sightings of a phantasmal child in the projection room.

For more than five years I drove past Alamo Quarry Plaza, intrigued by the striking smokestacks, but I had not had the opportunity to visit it until July 3, 2014, on my way back from investigating a nearby site. It was a blazingly hot day and I staggered around taking pictures, not so much conducting an investigation as just trying to get a sense for the place. When I finally accomplished all that I reasonably could, I moved on to the theater and obtained entry to it in the easiest and most unobtrusive way possible: I bought a ticket to a movie. Initially I planned on seeing *Transformers: Age of Extinction,* but, remembering how execrable its predecessor had been, was more than open to other options and would have preferred something more thematically appropriate. *Tammy, 22 Jump Street,* and *Think Like a Man 2* just weren't going to happen. *Maleficent* was getting a little closer but was not quite there. And then I spotted *Deliver Us from Evil.*

I was pleased to discover that my film was showing not just on the reputedly haunted second level but also at the very far end of a long, dark corridor. In retrospect, however, this creepy occult thriller based on ostensibly real events, as good as it is, may not have been the best choice and did not help with the less-than-optimum conditions under which I was operating.

I made a point of arriving about half an hour before the film started so that I would have a little time to make some observations, but I had decided not to bring my camera in with me, cinemas often being sensitive about such things. There were only a few people in the theater when I got there, however, and I probably would not have had any trouble doing a decent photo shoot of the area without attracting undue attention from the management. As it was, I did not see anything with my naked eye before the film began—and, of course, once it did begin, it was easy to see all sorts of things in the darkness after glancing away from the screen, especially one filled with scenes of demonic possession and other horrors.

It did, undeniably, feel unnaturally cold in the theater. I had, however, spent several hours that day walking around in the overwhelming Texas heat and gotten borderline dehydrated and a bit lightheaded. So, both the frigid temperature and my otherworldly feeling were all pretty much to be expected.

There was practically no chance at all of capturing any kind of paranormal audio phenomena like EVPs, because the whole theater was pretty much awash with anomalies. This included noise bleed from films showing in other parts of the building and horrible static during the pre-film attractions that was, according the manager, caused by problems with the signal being used to stream it. And, ironically enough, a plot point of the film was phantom noises that one character could hear but that no one else could!

Every investigation, of course, no matter how structured or casual, does not result in evidence of haunting or other paranormal phenomena. Sometimes it is enough just to enjoy the history of a place. Alamo Quarry Market affords ample opportunity for that as well as a chance to satisfy the shoppers in your group and get a decent meal at any number of places—and, of course, to see a good film if one happens to be showing when you are there.

CHAPTER 4

Comanche Lookout Park
NORTHEAST SAN ANTONIO

ALTHOUGH ONE OF SAN ANTONIO'S smaller
municipal parks, 96-acre Comanche Lookout Park emits a sense
of being a microcosm and frequently seems more isolated than
it really is, despite being surrounded by major roads, shopping

plazas, and housing developments. Those who visit it during normal business hours are likely to get an accentuated feel of this and, other than a few headphone-wearing people who jog by wraithlike and without acknowledgement, are likely to have the place pretty much to themselves. That, of course, can be the best way to explore and appreciate this profoundly historical site, to investigate the legends associated with it, and to possibly come into contact with some of the many ghosts who have long been believed to haunt it. And, as strange and haunting as it might feel on its face to the casual visitor or ghosthunter, an investigation of its history will reveal some genuinely strange things about it.

At 1,340 feet above sea level, what is also sometimes known as Comanche Hill is the highest point in northeastern Bexar County, at one time offering unobstructed views of the surrounding countryside. Only sporadic peeks are now available through gaps in the dense forest of native ash juniper, chinaberry, graneno, honey mesquite, huisache Lindheimer hackberry, live oak, and Texas and Mexican buckeye covering the slopes of the hill. At the time that what is now San Antonio was settled by Spanish colonists, however, the south Texas plains to the south and east and the hills of the Edwards Plateau rising up to the north and west were predominantly grasslands over which buffalo roamed. This ecosystem was maintained by immense fires that would periodically break out along the Gulf Coast and work their way northward over a period of months, killing any saplings that had sprouted up since the last conflagration swept through. Modern fire protection, roads, and infrastructure have greatly reduced the impact of these wildfires and allowed for the succession of forests in areas, including Texas Hill Country, that were formerly seas of grass.

Like many places in Texas where people lived at the time of initial European contact, what became known as the Comanche

Lookout was at least sporadically inhabited since prehistoric times by Paleo-Indians from no later than about 9500 B.C. onward.

In the 1700s and 1800s, Apache and then Comanche Indians hunted along nearby waterways that included seasonal Cibolo Creek, and used the hill both as a meeting place and a lookout from which they could scan the landscape for game. When Spanish colonists began traveling from Nacogdoches in east Texas for purposes of settling along the banks of the San Antonio River, the Comanches were able to spot them as well from the crest of the hill. This allowed the Indians to muster war bands in the hours before travelers arrived and to ambush them as they passed by the base of the hill along what was then known as the Camino Real—the "Royal Road"—and what is now known as Nacogdoches Road, a route that followed traditional Indian trails. The hill thus became a prominent landmark that told travelers not just that they were nearing their destination but also that they might soon be exposed to mortal danger as they completed the last leg of their journey, between Bastrop and San Antonio. Significant bloodshed occurred in the vicinity of the hill and continued to one extent or another into the 1870s.

The land surrounding and including Comanche Hill was part of a 1,476-acre land grant surveyed for owner James Conn in April 1847, and over the following 17 months the property was transferred to a number of other owners, including Peter W. Gray, a lawyer, legislator, and officer in the Texas Army; Alexander Patrick; and Ludovic Colquhoun, a surveyor and state senator. Frequent sale of land grants was not uncommon during the period of the Republic of Texas, so this is not overly exceptional in and of itself. This was also, however, the era of the bloody Indian Wars, and it bears asking whether either physical threat or the lingering spiritual energies of a site that had been used since time immemorial might not have played a role in these very short periods of ownership.

In September 1848, Mirabeau B. Lamar, a career diplomat, soldier, and politician who served as the second president of the Republic of Texas, acquired the property containing the Comanche Lookout. Exactly why he purchased it is unclear, and he appears to have not put it to any use during the remaining 11 years of his life. It passed to his daughter, Loretto Evalina, who was only 7 years old at the time of his death in 1859. She ultimately married Samuel Douglass Calder, member of another prominent Texas family, and they lived in Galveston and apparently did not use the property for anything, either. In July 1890, the Calders sold 524.6 acres of the land for $3,500 to brothers Gustav and Adolph Reeh, a pair of German immigrants who lived in Bexar County and used the land for farming. Then, in February 1923, following the death of Adolph, Gustav sold a part of the land containing the hill to retired U.S. Army Colonel Edward H. Coppock for $6,000.

Coppock was a 44-year veteran of the service who had fought in the wars against the Apache and Sioux, the Spanish-American War, the Philippine Insurrection, and World War I. He was also a history aficionado and romantic who had spent time in Europe and who had decided that he was going to build a full-sized, U-shaped castle on the slopes and flat crown of Comanche Hill. With help from his two sons, Edward Jr. and E. S., and a Mexican laborer named Tarquino Cavazos about which little else is known, he began to lay the foundations for and construct what was clearly intended to be a sprawling complex.

By 1928, they had completed the four-story, Norman-style stone tower that can be seen on the hill today and which was modeled after "a similar structure erected by William the Conqueror at the site of the Battle of Hastings in the 11th century," according to a 1948 newspaper article. In addition to this, over the 25 years that Coppock developed the property they also built a stone lodge, several outbuildings, a 2,500-gallon water tower, a Spanish-style corral, picnic tables, a barbecue pit, a tennis court,

and some smaller homes since destroyed by fire. Both Coppock and Cavazos died in 1948, however. The colonel's sons then abandoned the project and in 1968 sold the land to a developer.

Initially, the new owner began to move ahead with plans to develop the land and started by removing all of the structures on the property except for the tower and some of the foundations. For whatever reasons, however, they did not move ahead with any new construction and nothing was ever again built on or right around the hill. The property continued to change hands over the following years until, in the 1980s, the owner became insolvent and had to liquidate its assets, which led to acquisition of the property by the U.S. government's Resolution Trust Corporation in 1990.

Around this time a private group called Save Comanche Lookout led an effort to preserve the site that resulted in the Trust for Public Lands providing an interim loan to the city of San Antonio to purchase the site for a park. A 1994 bond issue provided the funds to repay this loan and develop the site.

"In 1995, the Parks and Recreation Department retained landscape architectural consultant Laffoon Associates to analyze the site and develop a conceptual plan that would preserve the park's natural and cultural assets," the city's official description of the site says. The first phase of development included construction of off-street parking, service roads, some trails, and installation of drinking fountains. The second phase of development was funded with $762,300 from a 1999 bond election and was completed in conjunction with construction of a branch library on the perimeter of the park, additional parking improvements and trails, picnic and restroom facilities, and landscaping. In 2004–05, the San Antonio Parks Foundation contributed $100,000 for an outdoor classroom.

IT WAS DURING THIS PERIOD that the Center for Archaeological Research at the University of Texas at San Antonio released, in 1998, "An Archaeological Investigation of Comanche Lookout Park." Suffice it to say that this report reveals some interesting things about the history and prehistory of the hill and the area surrounding it, including the presence of an ancient chert quarry, toolmaking area, and campsite. What it does not say, however, is perhaps even more interesting, but we may never know what that is, and it is here that we encounter one of those rare glimpses of officialdom coming into contact with things so strange that they cannot credibly deny or reveal their existence. Three pages of this report have, in fact—pages 2, 18, and 19—been redacted because they contain what is described as "restricted information." This sensitive information is being withheld not by a government agency but rather by a public research university, and is not about a site in some hellhole like North Korea but rather one right in the middle of an urban area in the United States. Whatever those pages contain, whatever the investigators discovered at Comanche Lookout Hill, was, in short, deemed to be of a nature that had to be withheld from the public at large.

Over the years, visitors claim to have seen ghosts of many sorts in the area, in both the park itself and along adjacent Nacogdoches Road, to include those of Indians, soldiers, and settlers. People also report seeing the specter of an old man pushing a rock-filled wheelbarrow, and this has been identified as old Colonel Coppock himself, trying in death to complete what he was so passionate about in life. His unquiet spirit is quite possibly also indignant about the people who have vandalized his tower, thrown rowdy parties in and around it, and even held rituals at it for purposes of calling up the shades of the dead. There are also vague and largely unsubstantiated rumors of gold buried on the hill and of Mormon settlers massacred near it.

One of the more dramatic episodes that has reportedly occurred at Comanche Lookout Park is described by Lauren M. and James A. Swartz in their book *Haunted History of Old San Antonio*. A woman they interviewed took a walk with her dog up to the top of the hill each day and, in the course of it, often heard chanting or voices in the forest around her but dismissed them as kids messing around. The last time she dared to go into the park, however, she had descended about halfway back down when it grew unnaturally dark and she spotted two strange-looking men with painted faces following her. When they screamed and charged her, she and her dog turned and fled, running as fast as they could back to the parking lot at the bottom of hill. She turned to face her attackers, but, as quickly as they had appeared, they were gone. She left as well and vowed to never again return to the park, believing that she had encountered the spirits of Native American warriors.

With its strange little trails leading off through the dense fragrant woods, medieval tower and ruined walls, and concealed history, Comanche Lookout Park certainly does have an otherworldly feel to it—the kind of place where something like this could happen. If there is anywhere one might expect an investigation to reveal evidence of paranormal activity it is certainly here.

CHAPTER 5

Crockett Hotel

DOWNTOWN SAN ANTONIO

ONE OF THE OLDEST HOSPITALITY establishments in San Antonio, the historic Crockett Hotel is also one of the most haunted and has a wealth of ghostly lore and paranormal phenomena associated with it. When one considers where it is located, of course, this is not overly surprising. The Crockett Hotel is right across the street from the Alamo, is located on the grounds of the battle that centered on it, and can often be spotted in photos of the famous mission or news stories about it. It is, in fact, believed to be built on the very spot where David Crockett and the last of the Alamo defenders were killed, on what had been the southeast palisade of the fortified mission. Crockett was one of at least 189 Texian revolutionaries who were ultimately overrun and killed by some 1,800 Mexican troops under the command of General Antonio López de Santa Anna at the end of a 13-day battle that ended on March 6, 1836.

For many years following the Battle of the Alamo, the site where the Crockett Hotel would eventually be built was simply used for farming, and the property changed hands numerous times. It was eventually acquired by a fraternal organization known as the Independent Order of Odd Fellows, which in 1877 erected a building on the site for use as a lodge. This structure served the organization well for more than three decades but, eventually, its members opted to create something bigger, and in 1909 they raised the current six-story building to serve both as a new fraternal lodge hotel and a lodge.

The seven-story west wing of the hotel was added 18 years later, in 1927. Other modifications made to the building over the following decades include the addition of a section of guestrooms to accommodate people attending the 1968 World's Fair. Time, however, eventually took a toll on the historic structure. In 1982, it was meticulously renovated to preserve its historic appearance and was added to the National Register of Historic Places by the U.S. Department of the Interior; it was eventually also added to the list of Historic Hotels of America by the National Trust for Historic Preservation. Then, in 2007, the Crockett Hotel was renovated once again and a number of dramatic changes were made, including restoration of the striking seventh-floor suites and removal of the rooms that had been added for the World's Fair so as to enhance the pool area.

The Crockett Hotel was, of course, named in honor of the man believed to have been killed on its grounds in the most famous battle in Texas history. It is also one of the relatively few sites where a credible case can be made for a haunting by a specific known person. Things that support the probability of this include it being the place of Crockett's violent and untimely death, his passion for Texas independence in life, and the site essentially being commemorated to him.

"You may all go to hell, and I will go to Texas," was Crockett's definitive statement on his emigration to the Lone Star State, summing up a determination in life that some people believe has kept his spirit present in death. His resolution and that of his companions served as inspiration for the ongoing Texas Revolution, and, some six weeks later, cries of "Remember the Alamo" bolstered the victorious Texian forces at the Battle of San Jacinto, final conflict of the war, in what is now Houston.

Beyond Crockett himself, the hotel has long been believed to be haunted by the spirits of others who fought and died in the Battle of the Alamo, Texian settlers and Mexican soldiers alike, and people have noted many sorts of paranormal activity throughout the building. There are also stories about a housekeeper said to have been murdered by her jealous husband during the early days of the hotel and whose ghost is believed by some to haunt the Crockett Hotel.

Particular areas in the building where people have traditionally noted possibly supernatural phenomena include the bar, a number of the guest rooms, and the lobby, where the main doors sometimes open and close on their own. The number and variety of things guests and staff alike have reported experiencing throughout the hotel is striking and far exceeds what is typically found at most other reputedly haunted sites. These include the sound of disembodied footsteps and even horses' hooves, faint whispers, curtains moving on their own, air conditioning and other electrical equipment going off or on by themselves, strange chanting, the sound of doors opening and closing when no one is present and even when locked, the sudden appearance of cold spots, and even the apparition of a man in a dark-blue military-style jacket.

People also complain of problems with the elevators, including them going up and down on their own, opening on floors
people had not pressed the buttons for and where no one was
waiting, and abruptly shifting floors after stopping. It is this
anomaly that led to a very recent tragedy at the hotel and, according to some, the possible addition of a new ghost to it.

On the evening of December 28, 2011, 65-year-old housekeeper Gloria Rodriguez was killed when she fell six floors
to the bottom of a service elevator shaft. According to Texas
Department of Licensing and Regulation chief inspector
Lawrence Taylor, what likely happened is that Rodriguez called
for the elevator and that it came up from a lower floor, caused
the doors for it to open, but then continued up to the next level.
When they did open, Rodriguez, unaware that the elevator car
itself was actually on the floor above, backed through them with
her cleaning cart and plummeted to her death at the bottom of
the shaft.

According to people who knew Rodriguez, she claimed to
have seen ghosts on a number of occasions at the Crockett,
where she had started working 12 years earlier, in 1999. She was
not the only person who believed the hotel was haunted.

"You should be scared, *mija,* this hotel is haunted," a housekeeper named Yolanda reportedly told a former front desk clerk
named Rosalie who expressed apprehensions about working in
the hotel at night and said she felt as though some dreadful
presence were watching her. Yolanda said many other people
had experienced supernatural things at the hotel and that Rodriguez in particular believed she could hear ghosts whispering in
the elevator shaft where she ultimately died. "Everyone knows
we're haunted now. She told us that's where the voices come
from, in there."

"No one will use that elevator anymore," Yolanda continued.
"Us girls are too scared. It's where she heard a lot of voices. No

one believed her, but now we do. She got worse toward the end. She was terrified of that elevator, but still no one believed her. No one wants to take that elevator, and I don't blame them."

For better or worse, visitors to the hotel will not likely have access to the elevator in question. But, like many hotels, the Crockett is ideal for an investigation, and a casual one might be possible even for visitors who are not guests of the hotel but who behave both subtly and responsibly. It should, in fact, be considered for inclusion in any investigation of the Alamo itself, and is in many ways more accessible, especially for those who prefer nighttime ghosthunts and opt to stay at the hotel.

When my wife and I visited the Crockett Hotel in the course of doing research for this book in January 2014, we had no trouble thoroughly photographing the lobby and adjacent areas (or, naturally, the exterior of the hotel). We then spent a few hours in the hotel bar, conducting a mini-investigation of it and chatting with the bartender, who was quite outspoken about inexplicable things she had experienced at the Crockett and ones she had heard about from others. In addition to the anomalies commonly associated with the site, she mentioned items flinging themselves off the bar and from counter surfaces in the kitchen.

So, if you find yourself in San Antonio, especially if you are conducting a paranormal investigation of the Alamo, there is no better place to both stay and look for local ghosts than the Crockett Hotel. Even if you cannot stay the night, stop by the bar for a drink. You may just notice something ever so small that lets you know you are in the presence of David Crockett, Gloria Rodriguez, or one of the other people whose lives ended here but whose spirits might still haunt it.

CHAPTER 6

Emily Morgan Hotel
DOWNTOWN SAN ANTONIO

LOCATED IN ONE OF THE LARGEST AND MOST imposing buildings in downtown San Antonio, the Emily Morgan Hotel is one of the city's quintessential lodgings—all the more so in that it is the "official hotel of the Alamo"—and at the same time stranger and much different from any of the others. Its merits as a beautiful luxury hotel aside, it has both a unique and atypical history and, as its namesake, the woman who may well have inspired the classic song "The Yellow Rose of Texas."

"The Emily Morgan Hotel was originally developed as a hospital, and then in 1984 it was converted into a hotel," Allison Schiess of the Sisters Grimm Ghost Tours told me. "It is named after the woman, an indentured servant, who was 'distracting' Santa Anna when the Texians attacked the Mexicans during the Battle of San Jacinto. So, she helped us win our independence."

The history of the building itself is interesting but fairly straightforward. However, the story behind its current namesake is equally fascinating and somewhat more complex.

In 1924, what is now the Emily Morgan Hotel opened as the Medical Arts Building. Noted architect Ralph Cameron designed the distinctive 13-story reinforced concrete Gothic Revival tower, a style popular for high-rise buildings during that era, and its ornamentation includes terra-cotta gargoyles depicting figures with toothaches and other medical ailments. It is distinguished by a glazed terra-cotta exterior on its top three and bottom three levels and faced with light-colored brick on its intervening ones. The marquee over its main entrance and the panels between its first and second levels are made of cast iron painted to simulate bronze, while its roof is fashioned from wooden ribs covered with copper.

In 1976, the former medical building was converted into a modern office building and then, eight years later, retrofitted once again and opened as the Emily Morgan Hotel. It is listed in the National Register of Historic Places as part of Alamo Plaza, and in December 2012 became part of the DoubleTree by Hilton organization.

Emily Morgan, the woman for whom the hotel in San Antonio is named, has a somewhat more complex history. Everything, in fact, from her very name, to the role she played during the Texas Revolution, to whether or not she is the subject of the state's most iconic song is the subject of some dispute. Some sources hold that she was a veritable Texas Mata Hari at the one extreme, while others dismiss her as a pawn of circumstances and try to ignore her entirely. As is often the case, the truth probably lies somewhere in between.

Emily D. West (c. 1815–1891) was a free woman of color, "high yellow" in the parlance of the day, who was born in New Haven, Connecticut. In 1835, when she was about 20 years old, West was contracted by Colonel James Morgan of New York to work as an indentured servant for a year—and, following the custom of the era, was supposed to have taken the surname of her patron. She was, accordingly, sent to serve as a housekeeper at the New Washington Association's hotel in Morgan's Point, Texas, on the shores of Galveston Bay and not far from what is now Houston.

In the meantime, war broke out in the region in October 1835 with the start of the Texas Revolution. Thus it was that on April 16, 1836, several months into her term of service, the woman known as Emily Morgan was captured by Mexican troops and, along with other local people, forced to travel with the forces of General Antonio López de Santa Anna. This led to her being in the Mexican army camp at Buffalo Bayou, at a spot in what is now the city of Houston, on April 21, six weeks after the fall of the Alamo. There, Santa Anna was preparing to face forces under the command of Sam Houston and expected to achieve yet another victory and put down the revolution once and for all.

According to legend, the attractive Morgan was in bed with and entertaining the womanizing *generalissimo* during his afternoon siesta (some variants include her merely dancing for him, while others go so far as to have her actually drugging him). Commander and men alike were caught off guard when the Texians attacked, savagely defeating the Mexicans in minutes at what became known as the Battle of San Jacinto, bringing the war to an end and permitting the formation of an independent Republic of Texas. Santa Anna fled and was found hiding under a tree clad in a dressing gown and slippers (attire that sparked rumors among the rugged Texians that the Mexican commander had tried to escaped disguised as a woman).

"The Battle of San Jacinto was probably lost to the Mexicans owing to the influence of a mulatto girl belonging to Colonel Morgan, who was closeted in the tent with General Santa [Anna], at the time cry was made, 'The enemy! They come! They come!'" wrote British diarist William Bollaert. "She delayed Santa [Anna] so long that order could not be restored readily again."

Because of her reputed beauty and ostensible role in keeping the brutal and womanizing Santa Anna from paying due attention to his military responsibilities, Morgan also has been identified by many as the woman immortalized in "The Yellow Rose of Texas." The song appears, in fact, to have been written in 1836 and the original version does indeed describe its subject as "the sweetest rose of color."

Whatever role she might have played in the triumph of the Texian revolutionaries, Morgan wanted to leave Texas after the Battle of San Jacinto. She had, however, lost the documents indicating she was free when she was captured by the Mexicans, and in this era of slavery was therefore unable to obtain a passport so that she could travel back to the United States. Morgan was eventually able to overcome this when Major Isaac Moreland, commandant of the Texas military garrison at Galveston, vouched for her, and it appears that she took passage back to New York in March 1837.

Emily Morgan is, in any event, an appropriate namesake for a grand and mysterious hotel that is, by all accounts, haunted and where people have experienced many profound paranormal phenomena.

"The building has 13 floors, but because 13 is considered to be unlucky, the numbering on the floors goes from 12 to 14," Allison Schiess told me (a practice common in many tall buildings). "The 12th floor was the operating level. People will see nurses appear in the hallways pushing gurneys and then disappear. They also say that they get touched by something when no one is there. The swimming pool is constructed out of stainless steel taken from the old hospital operating tables, and the 14th floor still smells exactly like a hospital to this day."

Olfactory phenomena, for some reason more often reported in hotels than anywhere else, are indeed one of the characteristics of the Emily Morgan.

"A morgue and a crematory were in the basement, and people will hear voices and footsteps and can still smell the scent of the bodies being burned," Schiess said. She added that she has personally experienced going from floor to floor of the hotel and discovering that each had a completely different odor to it. Furthermore, she told me, she has found that individuals within the same group will each smell different things on various floors. When friends visit from out of town, she said, she likes to bring them to the Emily Morgan so that they can experience this.

Not all the supernatural things people claim to have witnessed at the Emily Morgan Hotel are quite so innocuous as inexplicable scents. One woman described a very graphic experience there to Schiess.

"She saw blood appear on the walls in the bathrooms and when she went to tell her husband, they saw blood appear in their bed!" Schiess told me, noting that this episode had happened about two years earlier. The couple fled the room and the manager went up to investigate, but by the time he did, all the blood had disappeared.

Many other sorts of paranormal activity had been noted throughout the hotel. Schiess said, for example, that a ghostly bride haunts the seventh floor. Some visitors also say that the ninth floor is especially active and that things they experienced there include doors opening and closing all night long even though they were the only ones staying there; the toilet seat in their bathroom slamming itself up and down about 10 times; objects like a bottle of wine and a coffee pot sliding off a counter; and the elevator not stopping at the floor they wanted to get off on and, when it finally did, the door closing too quickly for them to get out of it.

As one of San Antonio's great downtown hotels, the Emily Morgan is certainly a great place to stay while visiting the city and its many historic sites. And, for paranormal investigators or those hoping to experience something that goes beyond the usual, this former hospital, tribute to one of the heroines of Texas history and haunted landmark, might be the place to find it.

"The Yellow Rose of Texas"

Anyone familiar with the lyrics of "The Yellow Rose of Texas" as they are sung today, based on an 1858 version of the song published in New York City, would not necessarily have reason to think they were inspired by the woman known as Emily Morgan. However, an unpublished handwritten version that may date to 1836, the year of the Battle of San Jacinto, while much less palatable to modern listeners, is also more explicit in references to the race of its subject:

> There's a yellow rose in Texas, that I am going to see,
> No other darky knows her, no darky only me
> She cryed so when I left her it like to broke my heart,
> And if I ever find her, we nevermore will part.

Chorus:
> She's the sweetest rose of color this darky ever knew,
> Her eyes are bright as diamonds, they sparkle like the dew;
> You may talk about your Dearest May, and sing of Rosa Lee,
> But the Yellow Rose of Texas is the only girl for me.
> When the Rio Grande is flowing, the starry skies are bright,
> She walks along the river in the quite [sic] summer night:
> She thinks if I remember, when we parted long ago,
> I promised to come back again, and not to leave her so.

[Repeat chorus]
> Oh now I'm going to find her, for my heart is full of woe,
> And we'll sing the songs togeather [sic], that we sung so long ago
> We'll play the bango gaily, and we'll sing the songs of yore,
> And the Yellow Rose of Texas shall be mine forevermore.

[Repeat chorus]

CHAPTER 7

Menger Hotel
DOWNTOWN SAN ANTONIO

IN AN OLD AND STORIED STATE OCCUPIED by the ghosts of a colorful and bloody past, one might think that the title "Most Haunted Hotel in Texas" would be a tough one to live up to. With some three dozen spirits identified in it, however, give or take a few, the sprawling Menger Hotel has a strong case for making this claim. These spirits reportedly include the ghosts of conquistadores, Indians, Texian and Mexican soldiers who fought in the Battle of the Alamo, cowboys who drove cattle on the Chisholm Trail, a land baron, a U.S. president, a murdered housekeeper, a "lady in blue," and a little girl who died by misfortune. As anyone investigating the site quickly learns, the mundane and supernatural histories of the hotel are inextricably linked and span the centuries.

In the 1850s, two of the most prominent businesspeople running establishments in San Antonio were German immigrant William Menger and his wife, Mary. They owned and operated the Western Brewery, the first commercial brewery in Texas, and next door to it a boarding house, both located right on Alamo Square and on ground where the most famous battle in Texas history was fought. The couple decided to replace the boarding house and support the brewery with a luxury hotel. On February 1, 1859, they opened the Menger Hotel, a two-story, 50-room limestone structure designed by local architect John M. Fries. Its features included classical elements like pilasters and a pediment, as well as a large, cool cellar with 3-foot-thick cut-stone walls that they used to store beer brewed in the adjacent facility. There was also a now-sealed tunnel to the Alamo, likely from an earlier era, and a 10- by 12-foot chamber cut into the bedrock beneath the cellar that was at some point fitted with a double-padlocked steel door.

The new hotel was an immediate success and within months the Mengers added a 40-room extension that included the Colonial Room restaurant.

Sam Houston, who served variously as president, governor, and senator from Texas, was one of the first prominent guests of the Menger Hotel and visited it shortly after it opened its doors, unquestionably an auspicious omen for its future.

Another early guest of the hotel who went on to achieve fame was Robert E. Lee, who came to Texas in 1860 as part of an effort to put down incursions by bandits from Mexico and stayed at the Menger several times.

"He rode his famous horse, Traveler, into the Menger lobby, and he placed a gold locket around the neck of the Mengers' young daughter, Catherine Barbara," the official history of the Menger Hotel states. This all seems a little ostentatious for a man who is perhaps best remembered for his humble and self-effacing nature, but maybe the blazing heat and open spaces of the Lone Star State affected him.

On March 28, 1876, an African American hotel maid named Sallie White was attacked by her jealous and violent husband, who gunned her down in the street a few blocks from the Menger. She lived for two days before finally succumbing to her wounds. The hotel took responsibility for her funeral and paid $7 for a coffin and $25 for a grave plot, as indicated by a receipt that is today displayed in the lobby of the hotel. Over the years, many people claimed to see the apparition of the unfortunate woman, carrying towels or performing other housekeeping duties, especially in the second-floor area, now known as the Roy Rogers Suite.

Also in 1876, the first-ever public demonstration of an innovative new product that would become closely identified with Texas—barbed wire—was held outside the Menger and orders were taken for it afterward inside the hotel. A prominent customer of that particular product was entrepreneur and Captain Richard King, founder of the fabled million-acre King Ranch in south Texas. A part-time resident of the Menger, King, in fact, spent enough time there that he had his own suite on the second floor overlooking Alamo Square. In 1885, he died of stomach cancer in his room at the Menger Hotel, and funeral services were held for him in the lobby. His chair and the very bed he died in remain in the King Suite and can be used by guests. His ghost is one that many people claim to see at the hotel—among them people who have awakened in the middle of the night to see the spectral cattle baron staring down at them from the foot of his bed! A strange red orb also has been seen in the room, particularly around the furniture associated with Captain King.

By the time the railroad arrived in San Antonio in 1877, the Menger was the best-known hotel in the Southwest, widely considered to be the finest west of the Mississippi River and the most popular in San Antonio. Both the hotel and its restaurant brought a sophistication to what was still a rough frontier area. For the next century and a half, it continued to be periodically enlarged or remodeled to accommodate more or better serve the needs of its guests and to intersect with historical people and events.

One of those episodes involved Apache war leader Geronimo, who surrendered to the U.S. Army in March 1886. He and some of his followers were thereafter transported to San Antonio and spent about six weeks there, imprisoned at nearby Fort Sam Houston, before being moved again. Local legend also maintains that Geronimo was kept for a short time in the vault beneath the cellar, and people who have worked near that section of the hotel have reportedly heard what have been characterized as "mournful chants." It is certainly possible, of course, that someone else altogether was imprisoned here at some point and that, their name lost to history, people have simply inserted a more familiar personage into their accounts.

A more verifiable visitor to the Menger Hotel was Theodore Roosevelt, who stayed at the hotel at least three times. The most famous of these stays occurred in 1898, on the eve of the Spanish-American War, when Roosevelt and U.S. Army Colonel Leonard Wood used the Menger Bar as a venue for recruiting the Rough Riders. This diverse volunteer regiment, which Roosevelt subsequently led in its famous charge up San Juan Hill in Cuba, was a virtual snapshot of Texas society and included cowboys, gamblers, prospectors, hunters, gamblers, Indians, and college students. Roosevelt returned to the Menger seven years later, in 1907, for the first Rough Rider reunion. In the century since that era, many people, especially employees who end up in the bar alone at night, claim that they have been approached by a strange man who has attempted to recruit them into Rough Riders. In some cases, this has caused such individuals to flee in fear when they realized they were dealing with a specter and, when other people returned to the bar to

investigate, there was no sign that anyone else had been there. Many people, in fact, believe that this is the ghost of Roosevelt himself. (This does not actually seem very likely to me, because Roosevelt went on to do many other things in his life and did not die anywhere near San Antonio, reducing any connections his spirit might have had with the site. It seems far more likely that this would be the ghost of a man who died during one of the battles in Cuba or who considered the episode to be the most significant of his life.)

In 1908, radical temperance movement crusader Carrie Nation came to San Antonio to preach against the evils of alcohol and, in the course of her stay, visited the Menger Bar to berate the bartender and customers. She apparently did not, however, attack the establishment with a hatchet, an act that she made her trademark. Fortunately, her unhappy and sanctimonious ghost is not among those believed to haunt the Menger Hotel. (Ten years later, however, Nation got her way throughout the country, and the hotel bar was one among the many that shut down during Prohibition.)

In 1909, noted architect Alfred Giles was contracted to implement extensive changes to the hotel, embellishing the original lobby with a new marble floor and Renaissance Revival–style details like filigreed balustrades and Corinthian columns. Then, in 1912, the hotel hired architect Atlee B. Ayres to add 30 rooms to the hotel and renovate the Colonial Room restaurant.

In 1924, noted sculptor Gutzon Borglum moved into the Menger and used his rooms there as a studio, planning and creating models for at least three of the presidential faces that appear on Mount Rushmore while staying there.

During the period 1949–1953, the Menger Hotel added a four-story, 125-room addition; a new lobby; and air-conditioning throughout the hotel. It moved the bar to its Crockett Street side and added a swimming pool and its Patio Club. In 1961–67 the hotel expanded yet again, building a five-story addition.

Even as the Menger Hotel has evolved, people have continued to stream through its doors from era to era.

Presidents of the United States other than Theodore Roosevelt who have stayed at the Menger, whether before or after their time in the White House, include Ulysses S. Grant, who stayed at the hotel during a visit to San Antonio in 1880; Benjamin Harrison; William McKinley; William H. Taft; Dwight D. Eisenhower, who visited first as a soldier in 1916 and later dined in the Colonial Room as president; and Richard M. Nixon.

A number of prominent writers also have visited the Menger Hotel over the years or have been known to frequent its bar or restaurant. These include flamboyant playwright Oscar Wilde, who traveled through San Antonio during a year-long tour of the United States; Sidney Lanier, who traveled to Texas during the bleak post–Civil War years of Reconstruction; and author William Sydney Porter (a.k.a. O. Henry), who spent time in Texas in the 1880s and mentions the Menger a number of times in his works. Because of this, the Menger Hotel was designated a Literary Landmark in 2000.

Other famous people who have stayed at the Menger Hotel include actors Sir Harry Lauder and Richard Mansfield and actresses Maude Adams, Sarah Bernhardt, Lillie Langtry, Anna

Held, Beverly Sills, and Mae West; U.S. Army generals John J. "Black Jack" Pershing and Phillip H. Sheridan; Texas Ranger Captain Leander McNelly; William F. "Buffalo Bill" Cody; baseball legend Babe Ruth; and tycoon Cornelius Vanderbilt. During the 1960s, Roy Rogers, his wife, Dale Evans, and their horse Trigger were also frequent guests at the Menger while performing in the Championship Rodeo at San Antonio—and a special hatch was built into one of the walls of their second-floor suite so that hotel staff could feed the horse without entering the rooms! It has since been sealed up but can still be seen in the hallway outside of what is now called the Roy Rogers Suite.

"[The Menger Hotel] witnessed exciting events preceding the Civil War, shared the tragedies of that war and bore the trials of Reconstruction, sheltered the various artists who contributed their talents to San Antonio's cultural growth, inspired writers, [and] honored military heroes and presidents," wrote Ella K. Dagget Stumpf in her 1952 book *San Antonio's Menger,* neatly summing up the place of the hotel in the city. "Its fortunes rose and fell and rose again with those of the citizens of San Antonio."

Today the Menger is almost as much a museum as it is a hotel, a 316-room composite of architectural styles that has been expanded over the span of three different centuries and is filled with antiques and other artifacts. Many people also have reason to believe that it is filled with ghosts. I had the opportunity to conduct an investigation at the hotel in January 2014. While I did not see any apparitions of buckskin-clad Alamo defenders or the like, I was intrigued by a number of anomalies that turned up in my photos and the possibility of paranormal activity that they suggested. If all that you experience during your own visit to the Menger Hotel is a glimpse into the history of a fascinating city and one of its most prominent establishments, then it will certainly be worth the time and effort. And there is always the chance that you will encounter much more.

CHAPTER 8

Old Bexar County Jail
DOWNTOWN SAN ANTONIO

PRESUMABLY, WE WILL NEVER see a commercial in which someone, when asked if they are a ghosthunter who spent the night in a haunted jail, replies with "No, but I did stay at a Holiday Inn Express last night!" On the other hand, it would be quite reasonable for someone to answer that question in the affirmative if they had just spent the night in the Holiday Inn Express Riverwalk Area, which is located in what was the Bexar County Jail for nearly a century.

By the late 1870s, Bexar County, the jurisdiction in which the city of San Antonio is located, needed a larger place to house its prisoners. At that point, any who were not summarily hanged were being kept in the jail the county had been using since Texas independence 40 years earlier, a basement facility colloquially known as the "Bat Cave." Accordingly, the county had a new, $34,000, 86-bed jail constructed at the corner of Camaron and Houston Streets, around the corner from City Hall, and demolished the decrepit original facility. Designed by prominent architect Alfred Giles, this two-story structure made from limestone blocks, which contained 20 cages for prisoners, was completed in 1879 and wryly nicknamed the "Shrimp Hotel" (*camarón* being the Spanish word for "shrimp").

Robbers, thieves, murderers, and lesser offenders were soon packed into the building more like sardines, however, and not too many years passed before the county needed to enlarge it. Architect Henry T. Phelps added a third floor to the jail and, in the course of this 1911–12 expansion, transformed it into the Mission Revival–style structure that it is today. He also added a rather strange feature to it, namely a gallows that had a hatch on the third floor and a viewing area for about 200 people, plus prisoners in the surrounding cages, on the second floor. When a condemned man was hanged at the jail, he would thus plummet down through the ceiling into the viewing area! His neck would snap when he reached the end of the rope, he would bounce back a bit on the taut line, and then he would dangle there until jailers lowered him to the floor.

Counties in Texas were responsible for carrying out executions until the 1920s, and they took place at the Bexar County

Jail until then. One of the last such executions was also of the person who perhaps, to date, committed the most gruesome murder the city of San Antonio has ever seen.

Apolinar Clemente had suffered a severe brain injury early in life that left him subject to symptoms like seizures, rage, paranoia, and hallucinations. On three previous occasions—in 1907, 1909, and 1916—he had been apprehended for various violations, found to be mentally incompetent, and committed to the Southwestern Insane Asylum in San Antonio. Every time, however, he escaped and went on to cause more trouble.

On August 16, 1921, 30-year-old Clemente was traveling by foot from Floresville to San Antonio, an all-day journey, when he stopped at a spring he knew near Salado Creek. Two young brothers, 14-year-old Theodore Bernhardt and 12-year-old Kirby Bernhardt, were playing nearby, and for whatever reasons Clemente became enraged and attacked them. He knocked the older one down and, as the younger one fled, broke his victim's head open with a large rock.

"Clemente was far from finished [and he] began to savagely mutilate the body," write Lauren and James Swartz in their *Haunted History of Old San Antonio*. "He took out his knife and cut the boy ear to ear, down the bridge of his nose and around to the back of the neck, even cutting open the top and back of his cranium. He continued by opening up the boy's head. With the lifeless corpse on its belly, Clemente began to remove the boy's brain, scooping it out and smashing it on his back until it was mush, leaving it there and even putting some in the boy's back pockets."

Clemente then cut off the boy's ears and gouged out one of his eyes. At least three people summoned by Kirby showed up to help but, horrified, retreated. When police caught up with the murderer, he was wandering through town, ranting, blood-spattered, and showing off Theodore Bernhardt's eye. He immediately declared to the officers that he was insane and that they therefore could not charge him with anything. They promptly arrested and threw him into the old Bexar County Jail to await trial.

Sadly, public opinion over what should happen to Clemente became divided along ethnic lines, with Anglo Americans generally thinking he should be put to death and Mexican Americans thinking he should be treated as mentally incompetent and allowed to live. For better or worse, Clemente was not tried by a jury of his peers, and a panel of 12 white men found him guilty, upon which the judge sentenced him to death. One can only imagine that they were impressed with some of Clemente's own testimony:

"I would have killed the other boy, too, if he wouldn't have gotten away!"

On February 23, 1923, Clemente became the first person in the history of the county to decline the option of wearing a black hood when he was hanged. An unforeseen side effect of this was that when he fell through the trapdoor in the jail there was no hood between his neck and the rope, which cut deeply into his flesh and nearly decapitated him. It also severed both his carotid artery and jugular vein, causing blood to spray witnesses up to 8 feet away. People screamed and ran for the doors.

All of this contributed to Clemente's role as a cause célèbre among the Hispanic community. More than 8,000 people attended his funeral, making it one of the biggest ever held in the city. (Anyone interested in visiting his grave can do so at San Fernando Cemetery I, just west of downtown San Antonio. More than a decade later, state and federal law enforcement officials operating under the assumption that Clemente was a habitual user of marijuana studied his case as an example of how dangerous the drug could be.)

As the community continued to grow over the following years, so did its need to house malefactors, and in 1926 the county added yet two more floors to its jail, bringing it up to a final total of five.

Father and son architects Atlee and Robert Ayres also faced the building in brick, reconfigured windows—many such openings being critical in a hot environment prior to the introduction of air conditioning—and added the facade and projecting arched entry-way over its main entrance that remain features to this day.

In this form, the jail served the needs of the county well enough for another three and a half decades. By 1962, however, overcrowding and poor food led to unrest in the facility, and at one point that year, 133 prisoners rioted, burning mattresses and demanding better provisions, prompting the guards to use fire hoses and wax bullets against them.

"This is no darn hotel," Sheriff William B. "Bill" Hauck said in a doubly ironic bit of foreshadowing. "If they don't like the meals we serve here, they can go somewhere else." In September of that year, the jail was finally shut down and the prisoners did indeed go somewhere else, namely to the new, 707-bed county detention facility four blocks away, at the corner of Nueva and Laredo streets. (After a few decades, this was itself too small to meet the needs of the county and also was shut down and in 1988 replaced with yet another facility, on Comal Street, the location of the Bexar County Jail today.)

For a time, the old Bexar County Jail was used as the county election center and archives building. Then, in 1983 a private company acquired the vacant building and renovated it for dedicated use as an archival storage facility. In December of that year, it also donated the historically significant facade of the structure to the San Antonio Conservation Society, transferring responsibility for this portion of the building to the preservation group. (The building overall is also listed on the National Register of Historic Places). Sometime after this, the building became a repository for county and city records and served in this capacity until 2000.

In 2002, Alamo City Hotels acquired the structure and set about renovating it while preserving its historic exterior, once

Lauren Swartz of Sisters Grimm ghost tours tells the story of Apolinar
Clemente and shows a picture of him while stopping with a group at the
Old Bexar County Jail/Holiday Inn Express Riverwalk Area.

again turning it into a place for people to stay, but this time not
as a jail. At this point the building also was repainted to empha-
size the brick detail on the facade. On November 26, 2004,
after a $6 million restoration, the 82-bed Comfort Inn Alamo/
Riverwalk opened to the public. (For sake of comparison, the jail
housed 328 prisoners on its last day of operation.)

"Guests have been thrilled about getting 'booked' into a
room," Omar Guevara, director of operations for Alamo City
Hotels, told the *San Antonio Current* soon after the hotel opened.
"Our desk clerks joke with the guests about being in jail. They
tell them 'You're our prisoner for the evening.' The original bars

can still be seen on the windows on the front facade and back side of the building, but have been removed from windows on guest rooms for safety reasons. And, while the hotel designed its lobby to look like the inside of a classic police station, it also added a heated swimming pool and hot tub, Internet and cable TV, refrigerators and microwaves in each room, a breakfast area, and a business center—amenities that would have been alien to the original inmates.

There are also reputedly any number of ghosts. This is only to be expected, of course, at a site where any number of people have been executed and where emotions, many of them very negative, have been experienced by thousands of people over the span of three centuries. Death, fear, despair, and similar conditions can go a long way toward promoting paranormal phenomena of the sorts so many people have reported at the site. One of the most common phenomena is that rooms remain unnaturally cold, even during the summer or if the heat is on. Other activity includes beds that are indented as if someone is lying on them but then the impressions abruptly disappear; people hearing whispering in their rooms that stops when the lights are turned on; objects being pulled out of people's hands and thrown across the room; and the breakfast area being rearranged and disheveled during the night. Most horrifying among the things people have reported, however, are in the rooms where the gallows were once located, where people claim to have seen apparitions fall through the ceiling as if just hanged!

Eventually, the Comfort Inn was replaced by the Holiday Inn Express that currently occupies the old Bexar County Jail. It is a nice hotel in a great location, and if you decide to stay at it, you should be sure to bask in the history of it and the surrounding neighborhood and to visit nearby sites of significance. But do not be surprised if you see any signs of supernatural activity—or even the deranged ghost of Apolinar Clemente himself.

CHAPTER 9

San Fernando Cathedral
DOWNTOWN SAN ANTONIO

IT WOULD NOT BE AN EXAGGERATION TO SAY that San Fernando Cathedral has, literally, been the spiritual and geographical heart of San Antonio for nearly 300 years, and there is even an official seal set into the floor of the church affirming this. It is, in fact, the oldest active Roman Catholic cathedral in Texas, one of the oldest in all of North America, and the mother church of the Archdiocese of San Antonio and seat of its archbishop.

As one of the oldest extant buildings in the city and the site of what most people today would consider to be some very strange practices, it is perhaps not too surprising that San Fernando Cathedral would have a reputation for spiritual activity. Phenomena people claim to witness at the site include spectral faces appearing on the walls and the apparition of a white horse galloping across the plaza in front of the church. Inside it definitely does, in any event, have a sacred and even otherworldly atmosphere.

I have visited San Fernando Cathedral a number of times and, most recently, had the privilege of doing so with Allison Schiess, one of the title members of Sisters Grimm Ghost Tours. She is a descendant of the Canary Islanders who built the church, and I very much enjoyed hearing her unique and personal perspectives on it.

In 1731, some 56 Canary Islanders arrived and settled in what would become the city of San Antonio, joining the Spanish military forces that had already occupied the area for 13 years. Seven years later, they broke ground on the church of San Fernando, overlooking the San Antonio River and near the presidio that would become the Spanish Governor's Palace (see Chapter 11). Progress on the church was slow, however, in part because of recurring attacks by the local Lipan Apache, who resented foreign settlement on lands they considered their own and waged war against the Spanish colonists for nearly two decades.

In 1749, the Apaches decided to make peace with the Spanish settlers and enacted an elaborate ritual to symbolize this. In front of the incomplete church, the Indians dug a great pit and placed axes, clubs, arrows, and other weapons and a living white horse in it, the animal representing the Apache's ability to wage war and its color symbolizing peace. Then, they literally "buried the hatchet," the origin of this phrase, filling in the pit and turning the horse into a living sacrifice. The Indians and the Spaniards concluded the ceremony by dancing around the pit.

It was probably increased peaceful contact with the Spaniards, rather than their gods being angry at them for concluding a treaty with their enemies, that soon after caused smallpox to break out amongst them. As the Indians had no resistance to this Old World disease, it wreaked havoc on them, and the survivors fled to escape it, ensuring even more conclusively than any treaty that they would no longer be a threat to the colony.

This peace allowed the settlers to make good progress on the church, and in just the following year, 1750, they finally completed it, naming it for 13th-century King Ferdinand III of Castile (although its official name to this day is Church of Nuestra Señora de la Candelaria y Guadalupe). The walls of that Spanish Colonial–style parish church form the sanctuary of the current cathedral, and this area contains a statue of the Virgin of Candelaria, patroness of the Canary Islands. Its baptismal font is believed to be a gift from King Charles III, who became King of Spain in 1759, and is the oldest item of liturgical furnishing in the cathedral. During the early years of the church, deceased parishioners were entombed within its walls.

In 1831, Anglo American trader and settler James Bowie married the socially prominent Ursula de Veramendi, a woman 20 years his junior who was the daughter of the governor of the Mexican state of Coahuila y Tejas, in San Fernando church. Despite his connections with the upper crust of local society, however, this joyous event set Bowie on a course that would lead to disease, drunkenness, and death—and, ultimately, a final return to the church. In 1833, a cholera epidemic swept through the region. Fearing for his family, Bowie sent them to the family

estate in the Mexican city of
Monclova, nearly 300 miles to
the southwest. Tragically, the
disease devastated that community, and, over an eight-
day period, it claimed Bowie's
wife, children, and in-laws.
He was never the same after
this. As he worked for Texas
independence over the following three years, his appearance slipped and he drank
heavily.

Five years after the ill-
fated nuptials, Mexican General Antonio López de Santa
Anna arrived in San Antonio
to put down the Texas Revolution and, when he besieged
the Alamo, hoisted a blood-red flag of "no quarter" from the
tower of San Fernando church. Thirteen days later, on March 6,
1836, Bowie was among the 189 Texians who died defending the
mission. His body was burned on a mass pyre; the ashes were
enclosed in a stone sepulchre marked with his name and those
of William Barret Travis and David Crockett and placed within
San Fernando church. It can be seen today in the front entryway
near the southeastern corner of the cathedral.

In 1868, the church was significantly expanded in the
Gothic style under the direction of architect Francois P. Giraud.
Six years later, when the Diocese of San Antonio was formed, the
church became a cathedral and the carved stone Stations of the
Cross were added. San Fernando Cathedral received its beautiful
stained glass windows in 1920.

San Fernando Cathedral remains at the heart of the Roman Catholic religious life of San Antonio to this day, with more than 5,000 people participating in masses each week and clergy performing some 900 baptisms, 100 weddings, 100 funerals, and innumerable other services each year. Special events include the annual Fiesta Week and staging of the Good Friday Passion Play, and, in 1975, it was added to the U.S. National Register of Historic Places. Pope John Paul II came to the cathedral in September 1987, during the only visit of a pope to Texas, an event commemorated with a marble stone marker. In 2003, a major three-phase, $15 million renovation project was undertaken at the cathedral that included the addition of a museum and gift shop and a radical rearrangement of liturgical elements like the altar and baptismal font. Then, in 2010, a new archbishop who was appointed by the pope undertook a renovation campaign of his own, reversing much of the vision from eight years earlier and restoring a more traditional arrangement of elements within his cathedral. He also placed three new relics—remains, generally pieces of bone from holy personages—in the altar.

As a place that people shed blood, sweat, and tears to erect, where every sort of emotion has been felt, the remains of people have been interred, and, indeed, living animals have been offered up the gods, it is little wonder that San Fernando Cathedral should be so spiritually charged. Innumerable people have reported supernatural experiences of various sorts at the church. These include orbs and other anomalies appearing in photographs of it, faces or skulls appearing in the plaster of its ancient walls, and even a spectral stallion galloping across the main square. You may or may not experience any of those things during your own visit to the cathedral—but you may very likely sense that it is possible.

CHAPTER 10

Sheraton Gunter Hotel San Antonio

DOWNTOWN SAN ANTONIO

SINCE 1837, TRAVELERS AND VISITORS to San Antonio have often found one of the nicest and most convenient hotels in the city to be located at a particular corner about 100 yards from the bank of the river. Over the years, this establishment has had many different names, occupied successively larger and more elaborate buildings, been controlled by the armies of four nations, and collectively contributed to a fascinating and colorful history. One of those colors, however, has been that of blood, and gruesome events that have occurred at the hotel are among the things that have led to it becoming a reputed venue for hauntings and paranormal activity.

"Just one year after the battle and fall of the Alamo, the Frontier Inn lit its kerosene lamps and opened its doors to the waves of new settlers surging in from the East," reads the history of the Sheraton Gunter Hotel San Antonio, which at first was situated at the corner of El Paso and El Rincón streets. "The inn had the best location in the center of a bustling town that sprawled comfortably along the banks of the winding San Antonio River." It survived two brief occupations of the city by invading Mexican troops trying to recapture the Republic of Texas in 1842.

In 1851, Irish immigrant brothers William, James, and John Vance bought the Frontier Hotel for $500 and replaced it with a two-story building on the corner of what had become Houston Street and St. Mary's Street. They leased this structure to the U.S. Army for use as its local headquarters until 1861. Then, when Texas seceded from the United States and joined the Confederate States of America in the months leading up to the Civil War, the U.S. Army withdrew from the city and C.S. military forces occupied it. The building changed hands again after the conflict ended. Federal troops occupied San Antonio and used the building until 1872, when they relinquished it back to the Vance brothers.

The building did not sit vacant long. That year its owners opened it as a fine hostelry that was known variously as the Vance House and Vance Hotel. This was a fortuitous and canny move and, when the first railroad arrived in San Antonio in 1877, its business doubled. Guests could travel by carriage from the train depot to the hotel for a nickel and, once there, enjoy first-class accommodations for $2 a day.

"We have another strictly first-class hotel, and very favorably located, handy for those who come here for business or for pleasure," travel writer Stephen Gould said in his *Alamo City Guide*. "Quiet and cool yet central, near all the churches, it combines all the elements needed in a hotel home."

In 1886, two men, German immigrant Ludwig Mahncke and Lesher A. Trexler, took over management of the hotel (although the property continued to be owned by the Vance family). Mahncke brought an Old World sensibility to the hotel, and Trexler, who was an experienced hotelier, knew how to attract both successful cattlemen and businessmen from throughout the region to their establishment, which they dubbed the Mahncke Hotel.

As the city moved into a new century and continued to thrive as a venue for business and tourism, a group of 13 local investors that included real estate developer L. J. Hart and rancher Jot Gunter formed the San Antonio Hotel Company. In 1907, they purchased from Mrs. Mary E. Vance Winslow for $190,000 the corner lot occupied by the Mahncke Hotel, razed it, and set out to erect in its place "a palatial structure that would meet the demands of the state's most progressive city." Gunter died before the project could be completed, however, and the hotel was therefore named in his honor.

On November 20, 1909, the Gunter Hotel opened in a new, eight-story, 301-room steel, concrete, and buff brick skyscraper designed by the St. Louis architectural firm of Mauran, Russell & Garden and built by the Westlake Construction Company. It was at that point the largest building ever raised in San Antonio. In 1917, it became even larger when a ninth story was added.

In 1924, the Baker Hotel Company purchased the hotel and two years later, under the direction of architect Herbert Green, expanded it yet again with the addition of three stories and, crowning a new annex, what was dubbed the "Gunter Roof."

On November 23, 1936, African American blues artist Robert Johnson participated in a historic recording session in room 414 of the Gunter. Talent scout H. C. Speir had arranged the session with Brunswick Records, which set up a temporary studio in the hotel where Johnson recorded a number of songs. Johnson was one of the most influential blues musicians of the era and the recordings he made in San Antonio remain significant to this day. He was so good for someone so young, in fact, that in some circles people genuinely believed he had made a classic cross-roads pact with the devil for success. His good fortune did not last much longer, however, and less than two years later he was dead, apparently poisoned by a jealous husband. Whether some of his spirit still lingers in the hotel is open to speculation, but in 2009, musician John Mellencamp felt compelled to come to the Gunter Hotel and record a new album of his own in the same room Johnson had used for these purposes.

It was in 1965 that the most terrible episode in the history of the hotel took place. On February 2 of that year, 37-year-old unemployed accountant and check forger Walter Emerick checked into room 636 of the Gunter Hotel under an assumed name. For three days, hotel staff saw him coming and going, at one point in the company of a tall blonde woman in her 30s. Then, on February 8, housekeeper Maria Luisa Leja entered the room to discover Emerick standing beside a blood-drenched bed. He held up a finger to his lips to enjoin her to silence. She screamed, and he darted past her and through the door clutching a bloodstained bundle.

When police arrived, they discovered that someone appeared to have been shot with a .22-caliber weapon in the room. The bathroom was covered in blood, and it appeared as if someone had been butchered in the bathtub and parts of them somehow flushed down the toilet. Police managed to track Emerick to the nearby St. Anthony Hotel. When they tried to apprehend him in his room there, he shot himself in the head with his .22-caliber handgun and died soon after.

Subsequent investigation revealed that Emerick had recently purchased a meat grinder and appeared to have shot, disarticulated, and ground up his blonde companion. She was never identified and no missing-person reports fitting her description turned up, so she was presumed to be a prostitute or someone else who would not be missed. Evidence suggested that Emerick had previously killed and disposed of other people in the same way.

Since that grisly incident, housekeeping staff and visitors alike have reported paranormal phenomena that include encounters with ghosts that could be those of Emerick and one or more of the people who died so horribly at his hands. In 1990, for example, a former hotel staff member named Jackie Contreras told paranormal researcher Docia Schultz Williams about entering a locked, darkened, and unoccupied room and encountering a disturbingly strange woman there.

"She was looking straight at me, her hands reaching toward me," Contreras said. "She looked very old and stooped and was white as a sheet. She was wearing a long white gown." Contreras quickly fled the room and said she believed she encountered a ghost and that she still felt chilled when she recalled the encounter. Others, including security personnel, have reported seeing apparitions at the Gunter Hotel as well, and people also have recounted things like hammering sounds coming from unoccupied rooms and ghost images turning up in photographs.

In the years following the murder in room 636, the hotel changed hands, form, and names a number of times. During the period 1980–1985, it was fully restored and a two-story parking garage added next door to it. In April 1986, it became the Radisson Gunter Hotel, in 1989 the Sheraton Gunter Hotel, in 1996 the Camberley Gunter Hotel, and, in 1999, following an $8 million restoration, it once again became the Sheraton Gunter Hotel San Antonio, the name it bears today. And on January 9, 2007, it was added to the U.S. National Register of Historic Places.

Whatever it is called and no matter how it is transformed over the decades, however, the Gunter Hotel's history remains the same, and it retains its role as a unique part of San Antonio's rich and multifaceted heritage. It also remains, with good reason, one of the most haunted hotels in the Alamo city.

CHAPTER 11

Spanish Governor's Palace
Downtown San Antonio

ONE OF THE OLDEST AND REPUTEDLY MOST
haunted places in a very old and haunted city is certainly the
Spanish Governor's Palace, which seems to have nearly as much
ghostly lore associated with it as the Alamo. I had the good fortune to visit this site for the first time in January 2014 in the
company of the knowledgeable Allison Schiess—a paranormal
investigator, one of the principals of Sisters Grimm Ghost Tours,
and the descendant of people who lived in San Antonio when the
palace was built—and learned quite a bit about it from her.

In 1718, Martín de Alarcón, governor of Coahuila and Texas,
established the Presidio San Antonio de Bexar to serve as the

center of Spanish military power in Texas and protect the San Antonio de Valero Mission (known later as the Alamo). This fortress was originally located a half mile west of the mission, but within four years Marqués de Aguayo had reestablished the presidio almost directly across the San Antonio River from it. By 1726, the total Spanish population of the area was about 200, including the 45 soldiers assigned to the presidio and their families living in the vicinity of it.

Plans for the house that became known as the Spanish Governor's Palace originated as early as 1722, and, upon its completion in 1749—the date given on the keystone bearing a carved, double-headed eagle that is above the front entrance—it served as the *commandancia*, the office and residence for the captain of the presidio.

By the 1760s, the presidio protected five missions and a civil settlement, the villa of San Fernando de Bexar, and also provided escorts for missionaries and other important officials and maintained regular communications among the disparate sites. It served as a strongpoint for the widespread community that would eventually form the basis for the city of San Antonio and more than once withstood assaults by raiding Indians.

In 1773, the importance of the presidio grew when the capital of Spanish Texas was moved to it from the presidio at Los Adaes, east of Nacogdoches, Texas. From this point onward, the Spanish governors stayed in the *commandancia*, and it was thereafter referred to as the Spanish Governor's Palace. As the seat of local government, justice was dispensed at the site, and some three dozen people convicted of criminal acts are known to have been hanged in the courtyard behind the building.

Throughout the early 1800s, the importance of Presidio San Antonio de Bexar declined and what was to become known as the Alamo eventually became the main bastion of defense in the area. It would remain so until the end of the Spanish and

Mexican eras in Texas. On June 4, 1836, the presidio ceased to exist as a military facility when the Mexican troops assigned to it recognized Texas as an independent state.

Ignatio Perez, a former Spanish governor of Texas, eventually purchased the Spanish Governor's Palace, and its title remained in his family until the late 1860s, when it was acquired by E. Hermann Altgelt, founder of the village of Comfort in Kendall County. Altgelt and his family lived in the house a number of times and his widow, Emma Murck Altgelt, owned it until the early 1900s, after which it fell into a state of disrepair. During this period, the function of the building shifted from residential to commercial, and a variety of establishments used its different rooms, including a tavern that sold nickel beer, a clothier, a produce market, a tailor shop, a pawn shop, and a school. By this era, people had begun to note supernatural activity of various sorts in the building, to include accounts of people seeing the ghosts of Spaniards, Indians, and hanged men, and it acquired a reputation for being haunted that persists to this day.

Then, in 1928, voters in San Antonio passed a bond issue for the purpose of purchasing and conserving the Spanish Governor's Palace, and the city acquired it later that year. Over the next three years, architect Harvey P. Smith supervised the restoration of the building, attempting to preserve as much of the original structure as possible, and in 1931 the city began operating it as a Museum of Spanish Colonial History. In 1962 the building was registered as a Texas Historic Landmark and in 1970 as a National Historic Landmark.

Today, the one-story building, a long, U-shaped stone structure covered in stucco that surrounds a traditional Spanish patio and courtyard, is the last visible trace of the presidio. It is the only remaining example in Texas of an aristocratic 18th-century Spanish Colonial townhouse, one of the oldest residential buildings still standing in Texas, and is maintained by the city of San

Antonio's Department for Culture and Creative Development as a public museum.

Numerous ghost stories and accounts of paranormal activity are associated with the site, many of them rooted in its Spanish Colonial history.

One of the most active areas is the beautiful garden located behind the courtyard, where what is known as the "Tree of Sorrows" is located and where at least 35 people were executed by hanging. Some paranormal investigators have reported seeing so many orbs around this location, possibly an indicator of a lingering spiritual presence of those who died here, that they looked almost as if they were there to decorate the tree.

At least two ghostly children are believed to haunt the Spanish Governor's Palace. One is the spirit of a little girl who resides in an area that appears to have been used at one point as a children's bedroom. Many people have reported feeling an unseen presence in this room, even before learning about the stories associated with it, and it frequently feels much colder in this area than in other sections of the house. Another little girl, reportedly related to the governor, is said to have drowned in the well of the courtyard, to have then been interred in the wall surrounding it, and to now haunt the area.

Another ghost who has been seen throughout the building is believed to be that of a governess for the governor's children who was killed and then thrown into the infamous well by brigands who broke into the home to rob it.

A lingering spirit with a less clear identity who has also been seen in the Spanish Governor's Palace, especially peering out of windows, has been dubbed the "Lady in Gray." She is said to have been a guest of the governor who arrived unannounced and then died mysteriously the very night she arrived.

A number of paranormal groups have conducted investigations of the site—something facilitated by the fact that it may be rented for special events that can include ghost hunts—including San Antonio Ghost Hunters, which posted a video of its investigation in July 2013. Among other things, they witnessed what they called "black mists," and what sounded an awful lot like what some paranormal investigators call "shadow people," moving around in the kitchen. They also captured several EVPs in the kitchen and bedroom areas, including both male and female voices, a woman saying "hate" and "get out," and what seemed to be another woman saying "hey" and "hello."

They said that the most active area during their investigation was the rear bedroom and that they photographed numerous orbs on and around the bed. Their video reveals the presence and movement of very small, bright anomalies.

Photographs I took during my own nighttime visit to the Spanish Governor's Palace revealed any number of things that could have been anomalies, especially several occurrences some might have taken to be faces manifesting themselves in the plaster of walls or peering out from the windows of darkened rooms. I am by now well accustomed to the vicissitudes of low light, dust-streaked glass, and the sorts of patterns that can seem to emerge from irregular surfaces of all sorts, however, and thus maintain a healthy skepticism when dealing with phenomena of this sort. Such images could indicate the presence of something or nothing at all, and, in the absence of other corroborating evidence, there is no way to know and nothing to be gained by assigning too much significance to them. Likewise, I did not detect in my recording of our visit anything that I would be confident in identifying as EVPs.

But I do not have much doubt that the Spanish Governor's Palace is haunted if anything is. It has every reason to be, and there is a wealth of lore and evidence to suggest this is the case. Whether you encounter or detect anything here during your own visit, however, you can hardly be disappointed by one of the oldest and most history-rich sites in the city of San Antonio.

CHAPTER 12

University of the Incarnate Word
ALAMO HEIGHTS/
MIDTOWN SAN ANTONIO

FOUNDED IN 1881 BY THE SISTERS of Charity of the Incarnate Word as a school for young women, the University of the Incarnate Word is one of the three oldest institutions of higher education in the city of San Antonio. It should thus come as no surprise that it is also one of the most haunted and that at least three of its buildings are believed to be inhabited by the spirits of those who have lived on the campus in years past. Beyond merely being haunted, however, some parts of the university feel almost mystical, from the resting place of nuns who lived out their lives there, to a holy grotto modeled after one of the most sacred in Europe, to the very headwaters of the San Antonio River.

In 1866, nuns from the Order of the Incarnate Word and Blessed Sacrament in Lyons, France, responded to a call from Bishop of Galveston Claude M. Dubuis to come to Texas and care for orphans and the sick. A group came and established a hospital and new congregation on Galveston Island. Then, in 1869, the bishop dispatched three of them—sisters St. Madeleine Chollet, St. Pierre Cinquin, and Agnes Buisson—to San Antonio for purposes of founding the first hospital in the area as part of fighting an outbreak of cholera. There they founded a new community and Santa Rosa Infirmary (the basis for what would eventually become the Christus Santa Rosa Health System), celebrating their first mass at it on December 3 of that year. Dubuis named Sister St. Madeleine as initial superior of the community, and she served in this capacity for its first three years, succeeded by Sister St. Pierre, who then served for the next 20 years. Three more nuns from Texas joined the congregation in 1871, and the following year they established St. Joseph's Orphanage and began their ministry of education.

Over the following decades, demands for the congregation to provide health care and education throughout the area, to include staffing railroad hospitals, expanded so rapidly that sisters began to actively recruit new members in France, Ireland, and Germany. In 1881, Texas Secretary of State Oran M. Roberts granted the congregation authorization to operate hospitals and schools within the state. The sisters proceeded that very year to found Incarnate Word School as an educational institution for women in a section of San Antonio known as Government Hill.

In 1890, as the congregation continued to expand to meet the needs of additional nuns and the indigent and orphans in their care, it established St. John's Orphanage in south San Antonio, using its upper two floors as a novitiate for training new sisters. Five years later, the sisters built a facility to accommodate aging and infirm members and support their ministry for elderly people in San Antonio. Around this time, they also mourned the deaths of Bishop Dubuis and Sister St. Pierre.

Then, in 1897, the congregation purchased the 283-acre estate at the headwaters of the San Antonio River known as Alamo Heights, an area that had been sacred to and inhabited by native peoples for some 7,000 years. City alderman and former mayor James R. Sweet had acquired the property from the city 45 years earlier and built the one-story house that sits there still, creating a firestorm of controversy when he established a waterworks company that gave him sole control over the city's water supply. Sweet sold the land in 1869 to Isabella Brackenridge, mother of George Washington Brackenridge, who named the house Fernridge and constructed a large Queen Anne–style mansion connected to the existing house by a breezeway. Its interior was distinguished by an eclectic mix of styles from her travels. The sisters moved their novitiate to the new property, which they called Brackenridge Villa, and used it as a temporary motherhouse for three years. In the meantime, they began construction on a dedicated motherhouse in 1898. In 1900, they completed and moved into it and relocated the high school from Government Hill to the new site.

The new motherhouse provided housing for the growing number of sisters, which was being augmented by members from throughout Europe, Canada, Mexico, and the United States, and also served as administrative offices and a dormitory for lay students. In 1907, the adjacent Chapel of the Incarnate Word was consecrated shortly after the death of Sister St. Madeleine. Then, in 1909, the order added college courses to the school's curriculum and renamed it the College and Academy of the Incarnate Word.

The decade of the 1910s was largely a turbulent and tragic one for the congregation. Many people from affiliated religious institutions were displaced by the Mexican Revolution and some of them stayed with the congregation for a time. In 1912, a fire destroyed St. John's Orphanage and killed five of the sisters and three children, and another seven of the nuns lost their lives in a series of subsequent calamities which included a massive hurricane that ravaged Galveston.

In 1919, the Sisters of Charity of the Incarnate Word celebrated their 50th anniversary. At that point they had 663 nuns working in 60 institutions, among them the college, 40 schools and academies, a dozen hospitals, four orphanages, and two homes for the elderly.

By that point, the college had become affiliated with the Texas State Department of Education, was granted membership in the Association of Colleges and Secondary Schools, became a senior college of the Texas Association of Colleges in 1920, and was fully accredited by the ACSC in 1925. A graduate studies program was established in 1950, male students were admitted in 1970, and the institution became the University of the Incarnate Word in 1996. Today, UIW serves more than 9,000 students on its 154-acre campus and is the largest Catholic university and the fourth-largest private university in Texas. With its long, colorful, and sometimes tumultuous history, and with all of the emotions and passions that the innumerable who have walked the campus have experienced, it is little wonder that many people consider it to be occupied by spiritual presences.

One of the buildings many people believe to be haunted is Bishop Claude M. Dubuis Residence Hall, a university dormitory for first-year students that was built in 1928. Students have reported experiencing uneasy feelings at night and expressed the sensation that they were being watched by the ghost of a nun. Perhaps they had reason, however, to not want to be watched and the spectral sister was simply continuing in death the vigilance she had practiced in life. Support for this supposition is suggested by the account of a female student who said she woke up one morning to discover that her stuffed animals had been completely rearranged and neatened up while she slept! This hardly seems to be the action of a malignant spirit.

Another one of the places on campus reputed to be haunted is the university's main Administration Building, which was completed in 1922. People have reported a number of oddities here, including inexplicable cold spots and radios scanning through stations on their own. This building's fourth and top floor was reportedly once used as a tuberculosis ward and therefore had been the scene of many unhappy deaths, something that could certainly account for ghostly presences. People also claim to have spotted on numerous occasions the apparition of a young boy about 5 years old chasing a bouncing ball on the third floor.

As the oldest structure on the campus, it is perhaps to be expected that Brackenridge Villa might be haunted. Once the sisters outgrew it and moved into the new dedicated motherhouse in 1900, this building was used, among other things, as accommodations for guests, and perhaps that is a key to the paranormal phenomena people have experienced there. Many clergy members had to flee Mexico during the period of its 1910–1920 revolution and seek shelter among congregations in other areas, to include the cloister of the Sisters of Charity of the Incarnate Word. Brackenridge Villa was thus the temporary home of any number of refugees whose future was by no means certain and who would have felt all sorts of powerful and, in many cases, negative emotions. Both the mansion and the homestead building were severely damaged by a fire in 1983, and have since been completely restored. These are, in any event, the very sorts of conditions that many paranormal researchers believe can lead to psychic imprints or lingering spiritual presences commonly known as hauntings. Recurring things that people have reported at this site include seeing strange, shadowy figures in its windows when it is closed up and no one is present in it.

There are also a number of sites on the University of the Incarnate Word campus where people have reported experiencing very positive spiritual feelings. All of these sites on the UIW campus are located on the short but fascinating CCVI Heritage Trail, and visitors can start at the oldest point on it, one that is deeply symbolic of life, and move on to the spot farthest from it, one equally emblematic of death.

At the western end of the trail is the Blue Hole, the mainspring of the San Antonio Springs, which rise up from the Edwards Aquifer and form the headwaters of the San Antonio River.

"The whole river gushes up in one sparkling burst from the earth," landscape architect Frederick Law Olmsted wrote of the site in 1857, which is now surrounded by a stone well wall. "Moss, pebbles, seclusion, sparkling sunbeams, dense overhanging luxuriant foliage . . . It is beyond your possible conceptions of a spring."

Sadly, while this spring used to flow perpetually, modern demands upon the aquifer now mean that it is completely dry during times of drought and that at such times no water at all is present in the narrow first stretch of the San Antonio River. (Much of the water that people see in the San Antonio River Walk, in fact, is provided by partially processed gray water from surrounding businesses.) When I visited the Blue Hole in early July 2014, I was able to look straight down into the rocky hole and see that it was completely dry, at least to the point where it disappeared into the darkness of the earth. One can only imagine how distressing this might be to any spirits associated with this once powerful natural phenomenon or those of the innumerable people who drew sustenance from it over untold millennia.

Moving south and generally eastward, visitors will soon come to the next point on the trail, a footbridge over the narrow bed of the San Antonio River. As noted, the bed of the river was completely dry during my visit but was nonetheless full of lush, junglelike plant growth. Up until the 1980s, the area to the west of the bridge was a wilderness area where sisters could walk among streams bubbling up from the ground, and a small dam created a spring-fed lake that they and students used as a recreation area. Today the area has been developed and is dominated by athletic facilities.

Next stop on the trail is the Lourdes Grotto, a replica of the shrine of Our Lady of Lourdes in France that was built in 1904.

"It is a special place for private and communal prayer and reflection," the trail sign says, and it is hard to see it and imagine otherwise. "After its dedication it became the focal point of processions on the principal Marian feast days."

Continuing generally eastward, trail followers first pass Brackenridge Villa and then the motherhouse, archives museum (which was closed for renovations during my visit), and chapel, all part of a sprawling and interconnected complex of stone-trimmed brick buildings. Then, moving around to the far side of these structures, visitors come to the final point on the heritage trail.

"Dedicated in 1928, Incarnate Word Cemetery is one of the numerous places where our Sisters are buried," the sign in front of the entrance reads. "The mortal remains of many of the early Sisters, including Rev. Mother Madeleine and Rev. Mother Pierre, were transferred here in 1930 from San Fernando Cemetery. This is holy ground and a place of prayer, where we honor and remember our 'great cloud of witnesses'—those who have gone before us."

And so it is that those who visit University of the Incarnate Word may indeed discover that it is a place where a supernatural presence might be felt and, perhaps, even detected. They might also come away with the impression, however, that whatever is present might, by and large, be more positively spiritual than what people might expect to find at many other haunted sites.

CHAPTER 13

Victoria's Black Swan Inn
NORTHEAST SAN ANTONIO

BUILT IN THE LATE 19TH CENTURY on the site of a battlefield where Texians fought to maintain the independence of their short-lived republic, the mansion now known as Victoria's Black Swan Inn is one of the most historic and haunted places in San Antonio. It is also one of the most famous sites of paranormal activity in the area, has been featured in numerous books, articles, and television programs on the paranormal, and is a popular venue for ghosthunting groups. One of those is the local San Antonio Ghost Hunters, and I had an opportunity to visit the inn for the first time in June 2014 as part of an overnight investigation with them.

On September 14, 1842, Texian and Mexican forces clashed on the site of the mansion in what became known as the Battle of Salado, so named for the creek that flows by in the valley below. This skirmish pitted a force of about 1,600 Mexican soldiers and Cherokee warriors under a French mercenary commander against some 200 Texas Rangers and militiamen, led in part by the famous Captain John C. "Jack" Hays. Making good use of the ridgeline where the mansion would eventually be built, the Texians achieved a decisive victory, killing or wounding some 60 Mexican troops while suffering one killed and nine wounded. This battle marked Mexico's final attempt to retake Texas, which had become an independent republic a little more than six years earlier (and would continue to be for another three years).

"The only Texian to die here on the property was named Steven Jett, who was killed going back to get his horse," Jo Ann Rivera, owner of Victoria's Black Swan Inn, told me during my visit. "He said his horse had gotten him out of a lot of bad places and that he wasn't going to leave him behind." She said that he is now one of the inn's resident ghosts. "He likes to bang the doors, shake the bed, and do pranky kinds of things. He likes women. We've gotten his voice lots of times on EVPs. He laughs, and he's got that old 'Heh heh heh' kind of laugh."

Forty-five years later, in 1887, a German immigrant couple named Heinrich and Marie Mahler purchased a 200-acre lot of land on the site of the battle and built a home on the bluff overlooking Salado Creek. In 1897, Mahler expanded his holdings by 240 acres and built a second home, a one-story farmhouse, on the knoll where Victoria's Black Swan Inn is now located. He used his property for ranching, farming crops that included cotton, and operating a dairy, and for years he sold his Jersey Creamery Butter to customers that included the Menger Hotel (see Chapter 7).

Heinrich died in 1923 at the age of 83 and left the portion of the farm containing the house, milk bark, and silo to his son Dan, who subsequently sold it to the Holbrook and Woods families. Those two couples, from Wichita Falls in north central Texas, were connected via their wives, Katherine Holbrook and Blanche Woods (née Joline). With an eye to cohabiting, the couples dramatically expanded the existing farmhouse, turning the main body of it into a single large drawing room that faced the front porch; built on each side of the building a long wing containing a large bedroom, a smaller bedroom, and a bathroom; and added to its back end a kitchen and dining room. They called their home White Gables.

John and Katherine Holbrook did not have any children. Claude and Blanche Woods had just one, a daughter named Joline, who married colorful and successful San Antonio attorney Hall Park Street Jr. In the 1940s and 1950s, they were among the most prominent members of the community, with Claude in particular having many professional and social honors bestowed upon him. After both the Holbrooks and Claude Woods passed away, the Streets and their two children moved into White Gables with the widowed Blanche. They added an upper level and expanded the house to 16 rooms and about 6,000 square feet of living space.

One of the guests in the elegant home on the hill was lawyer and author Erle Stanley Gardner, with home Street worked on a project called the "Court of Last Resort" that was intended to investigate and address miscarriages of justice. Gardner, in fact, dedicated his "Perry Mason" series of books to Street and is believed to have conceived several stories while visiting at White Gables. In 1959, Street held a dedication ceremony for the Perry

Mason room in his offices and flew in Gardner and TV show cast members Raymond Burr, Barbara Hale, William Hopper, William Talman, and Ray Collins for the celebration.

Tragedy descended on the family when Joline Street succumbed to cancer while only in her late 30s. Park Street eventually remarried but is believed to have never recovered emotionally from Joline's death and resided most of the time at the home of his new wife. He was found dead, apparently having committed suicide by strangling himself with a belt attached to a bedpost, on August 4, 1965, at age 55.

Street's daughter and her own family moved into White Gables with her grandmother until she finally passed away. It was during this era that residents of the house say they began to experience paranormal phenomena in it, to include feeling cold spots and hearing inexplicable noises. It is unclear whether that played a role in the family selling the home and abandoning many of their possessions when they moved out.

Whatever the case, a German woman named Ingebord Mehren, the wife of a former diplomat, purchased the home in 1973 with the intent of thoroughly renovating and making it available for conferences, dinners, luncheons, receptions, and other social events; she also put a significant amount of time and effort into sorting through, organizing, and disposing of the possessions that the Street family had abandoned in the house. Getting approval to use the property for commercial purposes took much longer than she had expected, so initially the house was unoccupied. After the house was broken into, vandalized, and robbed, however, Mrs. Mehren employed a series of resident caretakers to oversee it, and they began to report paranormal activity that went beyond anything people had claimed to experience at the house. One young couple reported seeing an apparition that fit the description of a young Joline Woods in 1920s-style apparel, and one man said he could not sleep in the house because it was occupied by so many spirits and that they made too much noise.

Mrs. Mehren was eventually able to begin hosting events at the house, and functions at what became known as Mehren House were noted for their European sophistication. People continued seeing and experiencing strange things during this period. On one occasion, two aristocratic friends of Mehren, one German and the other an Austrian who claimed to be psychically sensitive, said that several times they spotted the specter of an ugly, evil-looking old man. Whether episodes like this played a role in Mrs. Mehren's decision to sell the property and move on to other things is unclear, but in 1984, that is what she did.

The property changed hands a few more times over the following years until, in 1987, it was purchased by Jo Ann Rivera, the current owner, who lives in the house and has used it primarily for events like elegant wedding receptions. By that point it had acquired the name Black Swan Inn, after playwright William Shakespeare's favorite tavern, and as Rivera was making Victorian-era wedding dresses and crafts at the time, she appended "Victoria's" to it. Rivera also discovered early on that the place was haunted. In their 1993 book *Spirits of San Antonio and South Texas,* authors Docia Schultz Williams and Reneta Byrne devote several pages to describing Rivera's experiences during her first few years in the house. "[S]he was awakened at exactly 3 a.m. for about 10 nights straight," they write in one representative example. "Her bedroom door would unlock, and the lights in the hallway outside would switch on, and she would open her eyes to see a man, dressed in a white shirt and dark trousers, hands on his hips, standing at the foot of her bed. She was never able to get a good look at his face, and the apparition would disappear almost immediately as soon as she saw it. She was disturbed, to say the least! She finally repositioned her bed in the room, moving it to the other side, and since then the figure has not appeared, much to her relief."

Numerous other incidents are described in that book. They include Rivera's then-teenaged daughter seeing, peering at her through an upper-level bedroom window, the specter of an ugly, evil-looking old man that fit the description of the one the European visitors had seen years before! Other oddities include the piano in the parlor playing on its own, the sound of phantom hammering, and inexplicable cold spots—all things similar to those experienced by the Street family some two decades earlier. There were also episodes of doors locking or unlocking on their own, lights turning off or on for no apparent reason, and dolls being rearranged overnight as if someone had been playing with them.

It is thus not surprising that within just a few years of acquiring the property Rivera began making it available to paranormal investigators, to include a team of research scientists hosted by the University of Kentucky (who could not come to any definitive conclusions except that there was some sort of paranormal activity at the site).

"Sometimes it's pretty quiet," Rivera said to me while the San Antonio Ghost Hunters were getting their equipment set up. "Most times it's *very* active." According to Rivera, Victoria's Black Swan Inn is haunted by eight specific ghosts that have been identified, including those of Heinrich Mahler, especially outside of the old milking barn; a little girl named Sophie; John Holbrook; an unknown black woman in the house who seems to welcome visitors to it; and even Rivera's own mother, who lived in the house until she passed away unexpectedly in October 2012.

Rivera's mother made her presence known during filming for an episode of the *Ghost Adventures* reality show that aired in August 2013 when hosts Zak Bagans and Nick Groff insisted on trying to contact her. In the course of these attempts, what

Rivera believes was the spirit of her mother uttered a special code word she says only the two of them would have known.

"You could hear her," Rivera told me. "There were three of us in the room, and we each heard something different. Zak was insistent that he heard 'I love you.'" Rivera, however, was adamant that she heard something else, and when they played back the recording all three of them could clearly make out the word "Bossier." Bossier City, Louisiana, is the location of a casino that the older woman was planning on visiting for her birthday when she passed away unexpectedly, and this resonated strongly with Rivera.

Rivera said that there are also any number of other presences, including "travelers" who have no known connection to the place, who show up and stay for variable periods of time and are sometimes quite aggressive.

Why the site is such a magnet for ghosts and paranormal activity is a bit of a mystery. Some of the theories, however, are based on the property being situated on a limestone base and surrounded by two creeks, railway tracks, and radio towers, creating an ideal environment for the presence of spiritual energy.

"People have been investigating here for years and years now. It's kind of cool because it's helped us identify some of the spirits, because we have things to compare to, we can validate when they get things," Rivera said. There have, nonetheless, been a number of new and unexpected incidents at the house just recently.

"Last night there was a change in sorts of things I have been experiencing, and tonight we've had a lot of weird little things happening already," Rivera told me. "We had been out to dinner and I went to open the kitchen door. As I did, somebody shoved it back!" She thought it had been done by her friend, but when she opened the door, he was not there and so she challenged whatever was present to push the door again—and it did. "Then I got a really warm vibrational feeling and all the hair on my

arms stood up. The hair on my neck stood up, which was differ-ent. It was a change; it was somebody different."

Earlier that day Rivera received a series of panicked calls from a colleague who conducts daytime walking tours of the property. He had heard voices and the sound of a chair being dragged across the floor in the kitchen and assumed it was Rivera, but when he went in, he was shocked to discover she was not there. Then, a little later, he could feel what seemed to be heavy, booted steps walking across the sun porch!

Whether new spirits or just older and more familiar ones were among those that the San Antonio Ghost Hunters detected when they divided up into teams and began their investigation is not clear. Suffice it to say, however, that their efforts throughout the ground floor of the main house and in some of the outbuild-ings revealed a lot of activity.

Using "spirit boxes"—devices that create white noise that some people believe spirits can use as a medium for communication—San Antonio Ghost Hunters founder John Delgado and other members asked questions of any ghosts that might have been present. They got responses that included names that might have been those of the spirits responding and in some cases were certainly those of investigators present on the property, as well as utterances like "Get the f— out!" (something Rivera says she has experienced both audibly and in EVPs over the years).

San Antonio Ghost Hunters member Glenn Martinez also used a Kinect motion-sensing device for Xbox-system games in a very interesting and innovative way—to detect movement by things that might have been present but not visible. It was pretty amazing to be able to see the video image of a person on a laptop screen covered with the green lines that the Kinect system uses to model movement—and then to see next to them just green, disembodied stick figures that the ghosthunters took to be compelling evidence of a spiritual presence.

I personally experienced a number of strange things during my visit to Victoria's Black Swan Inn, albeit not ones I necessarily would have anticipated. In particular, with all of the activity being detected by the Kinect system, I really did expect to find significant anomalies in the photos I took of spots where it was showing presences and movement. While I did pick up some palpable orbs in a handful of pictures that I took outside, I could not find anything unexpected in any of my indoor shots. I did take a number of indoor photographs, which included mirrors or windows, and some of them did contain images that looked very much like demonic or skull-like faces; there was a similar effect in some fireplace ashes as well. It is all too easy, however, to make out faces and other patterns in old, murky, or dusty glass and, in the absence of some corroborating evidence, I tend to not take them too seriously.

There was, however, a very odd and somewhat disquieting effect on flash photographs I took in the mansion, especially in the main parlor, the area referred to as the Tea Room, and the attached scrying closet. On several occasions, the light from my flash was muted but not completely negated, as if about half of it had been absorbed, in three or four sequential images; by comparing images of the same objects without flash and in cases where the flash worked properly, I was able to see that these anomalous ones were somewhere in between.

Toward the end of the evening, those of us in the parlor also noticed on a number of occasions that people coming down the hall from the tea room were struggling to get through the door, which kept locking itself. The deadbolt mechanism was on our side of the room, but even after we would disengage it, we had some difficulty opening it for them. A person by themselves on the other side of the door certainly could have found this to be a very disquieting experience.

What is perhaps most amazing to me in retrospect is that paranormal activity would be so prolific, commonplace, and accepted at Victoria's Black Swan Inn, which makes it extraordinary in my experience. To detect anomalies or other evidence of spiritual activity at a reputedly haunted site more than about one time in 10 would be the exception to the rule. At this site, however, the proportions seem to be pretty much turned on their heads and the chances of experiencing some sort of phenomena more likely than not.

So, if you go to Victoria's Black Swan Inn, do not be surprised if you catch things in your photographs or recordings or even experience strange sights and sounds with your naked senses. But be careful if you do, because traveling spirits sometimes do move on and are sometimes inclined to do so with those who show a little too much interest in them.

Greater San Antonio

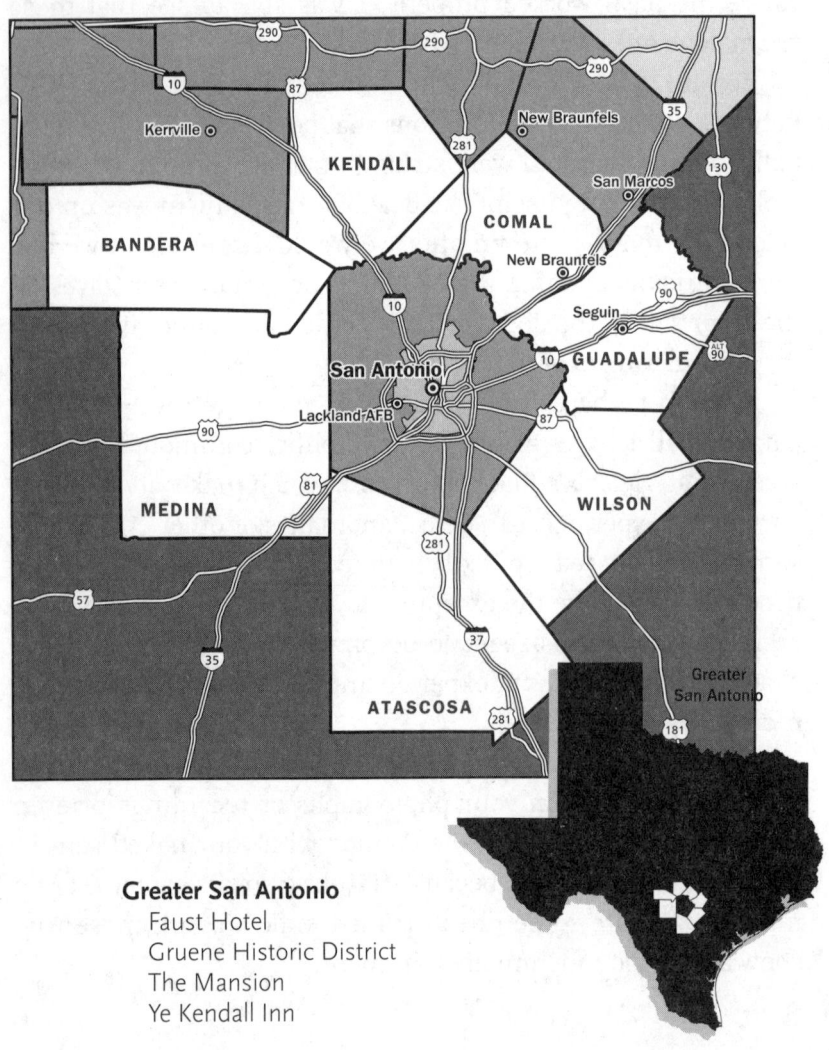

Greater San Antonio
Faust Hotel
Gruene Historic District
The Mansion
Ye Kendall Inn

CHAPTER 14

Faust Hotel
New Braunfels/Comal County

IN THE WESTERN LITERARY AND OCCULT tradi-
tions, the name "Faust" has an ominous connotation, and many
people assume that the historic hotel in New Braunfels bearing
this moniker received it as a tribute to the paranormal activity
associated with the site. It is, however, named for its founder,
flesh-and-blood local businessman Walter Faust Sr., rather than
a figure out of German legend.

Over the past few decades, the Faust Hotel has increasingly gained a widespread reputation for being haunted and
has attracted the attention of various paranormal investigative
groups. I have visited the hotel a number of times since 2009
and, among other things, have spent the night at it, conducted
investigations on or around Halloween twice, and appeared as
a guest on the PSI-FI Radio show while at it. It has, in fact,
become one of my favorite sites in the Greater San Antonio
area, not just for the strange things associated with it but also
for its colorful history.

In the years following World War I, community leaders in
New Braunfels decided that the town would benefit from the
presence of a luxury hotel. A local businessman named Walter
Faust Sr. took charge of the project, and what was initially known
as the Traveler's Hotel opened on October 12, 1929—just 17 days
before "Black Tuesday," the day the stock market crashed and the
start of what was to become known as the Great Depression.

It was, suffice it to say, about the worst time to try to make a
go of it with a luxury hotel. New Braunfels's economic woes were
exacerbated over the following years by the boll weevil blight, a
disaster that devastated cotton farming and crippled the local
textile industry. Faust was nonetheless determined to keep the
hotel open. During this period his establishment acquired a
reputation for being one of the best hotels in Texas and, being
located right across from a rail junction, a convenient place for
businessmen to meet. In 1936, it was renamed the Faust Hotel
in tribute to its founder.

During World War II, soldiers stationed at nearby military
bases took their sweethearts to the Faust before being shipped
overseas. As a result, New Braunfels became known in that era
as "the honeymoon capital of Texas," something that helped the
hotel stay in business.

Shortly after the war, the hotel was acquired by the politically connected Krueger family, but it declined over the following years and in 1975 closed its doors to guests. Two years later when Houstonite Steve Jackson purchased the property, its exterior had become blackened, many windows were broken out, the dining room floor had been ruined by water, and some furniture and most of the kitchen equipment had been stolen.

Its new owner fully renovated the establishment, however, and in 1978 reopened it as "the only full-service hotel in Texas that is also authentically restored to reflect its time of birth," according to *Texas Monthly* magazine. All 62 of its rooms were modernized and furnished with antiques like wardrobes, iron and mahogany bedsteads, and leather-topped writing desks. The Faust had been resurrected. In 1985, it became a Texas Historic Landmark and was added to the U.S. National Register of Historic Places.

In 2009, the Faust Hotel was acquired by Powerohm Properties, LLC, an affiliate of an electrical manufacturing company co-owned and managed by Vance Hinton of New Braunfels. His stated vision was to preserve the hotel and restore its historic 1930s-era ambience while incorporating modern amenities to maximize guest comfort, including repairing and bringing up to code all mechanical and electrical equipment and restoring the exterior of the building.

"Throughout the history of the Faust Hotel, most of the original furnishings disappeared and were replaced by a myriad of miscellaneous furnishings," the establishment's official history states. "The effort of outfitting each guest room with period antiques has proven to be challenging and time consuming, but the effort is ongoing and worthwhile." Even as it is being given a foothold in the past, the Faust is moving into the future, its rooms being outfitted with flat-screen televisions, new heating/air-conditioning units, and Wi-Fi.

I visited the Faust Hotel in New Braunfels for the first time around Halloween 2009 and heard tales about the ghosts that are said to inhabit it and the weird events that have happened in its Depression-era halls and rooms. Then, in 2011, I decided to check out the rumors for myself by spending the night at the Faust and conducting a paranormal investigation of it (a.k.a., a ghost hunt).

Supernatural phenomena reported at the hotel include seeing phantoms moving along the upstairs hallways, the lobby elevator inexplicably descending and opening on its own, and areas of intense cold air (phenomena I can confirm during my investigations as manifesting in the ground-floor men's restroom and the kitchen). Some postulate that it is haunted by the ghost of its former owner and namesake, Walter Faust Sr., who struggled so hard to keep it going during the tough years of the Great Depression.

Manager Doug Blank is well versed in the haunted history of the hotel, a popular venue for weddings and other special events, and each year he even gives ghost tours of the property to more than 2,000 fifth- and sixth-graders from around the area. He tries to reassure them, however, that they have nothing to fear as long as the gargoyle-faced fountain in the front of the hotel is flowing.

"This fountain had not worked for many, many years," Blank tells students on his tours. "Well, this guy was asleep. His eyes were actually closed for all those years. And when we blew him out and got the water running again, it seems like he woke up and we've never seen a haunted thing [since]. But beware if you come in here and he's not blowing water and he's asleep."

In January 2010, Blank said, he pulled up in front of the hotel and noticed that the gargoyle had frozen and stopped flowing, something it is only rarely cold enough for in the area. When he went into the hotel, he said, he discovered a guest wearing nothing but a towel who had panicked after getting out of the shower, discovering his wife was not in their room—but that there was a child's handprint in the steamed-up bathroom mirror!

Blank is ambiguous about whether or not he believes the hotel is actually haunted and has explanations for many of the phenomena people have reported in the historic establishment . . . sort of. He admits that it is not always in his interest for people to believe that the Faust is haunted, as in the multiple cases in which children have learned about the stories, become terrified, and induced their parents to decamp from the hotel just a few hours after checking in.

Knowing the stories, I checked into the Faust on the night of Wednesday, October 20, and specially requested the fourth floor, the one where most of the strange incidents have been reported. I was pleased to learn that my wife and I would be its sole occupants. (She was somewhat less pleased to learn this.) We were given room 406, the windows out of which the greatest number of spectral forms have been seen by people outside.

I also was intrigued to learn that a member of the housekeeping staff had recently seen a ghostly black cat leap from a table in the room onto the bed and then disappear! I spoke with her briefly and was impressed with her sincerity. Having an affinity for cats that they seem to reciprocate, I was not only unworried about a phantom feline, I was kind of hoping it might decide to sleep on our bed in the absence of our own cats back at home.

Unlike many paranormal investigators, I tend to go fairly light on equipment, preferring to use my own senses as my primary barometer for weirdness and supplementing them with only a digital camera, a digital recorder, and a flashlight. With just one night at my disposal, I decided to concentrate on a few specific areas of the hotel, namely the fourth floor and the elevator, which has a reputation for weird occurrences in particular.

Prowling the dimly lit, abandoned halls of the hotel in the middle of the night was a little spooky, but much less so than at many haunted places I have visited. I did not sense anything in particular and nothing turned up in any of the photographs I took to suggest I was missing something.

I also had my recorder going a lot of the time, both in the room and when I was on the move, in the hopes of capturing EVPs. These can be very disturbing, even frightening, especially because there is usually no audible evidence of their presence and they are thus revealed only by an examination of audio files or tapes after the fact.

The elevator, however, gave me a very bad vibe, and riding up and down in it and taking a series of photographs and recordings in two separate forays really gave me the creeps. One reason for this was some strange optical effect in which the mirrored side walls of the compartment did not have the typical, cascading-into-infinity effect, but rather swallowed up light like a void.

It was here that my photos did, in fact, reveal something! In a number of them, I picked up orbs, semisolid floating objects that cannot be seen with the naked eye but that turn up in images and tend to be indicators of ghostly activity. Whatever these were, they had been all around me when I was in the elevator taking pictures, and, even though I could not see them, they explained why the hair stood on the back of my neck the entire time.

So the Faust is indeed haunted, of that I am sure. Visit it next time you are passing through New Braunfels, have a microbrew beer made on the premises in its taproom, ride up and down the elevator a few times, and, if you can, spend the night and see if you experience anything for yourself.

CHAPTER 15

Gruene Historic District
NEW BRAUNFELS/COMAL COUNTY

ANYONE WHO HAS VISITED THE HISTORIC village
of Gruene on any given Saturday or any evening in the summer,
when it is thronged with tourists and local revelers alike, might be
surprised to learn that it was once a genuine ghost town. Gruene
was, however, virtually abandoned for more than two decades,
from around 1950 until the early 1970s, when it was restored
as a tourist attraction, and today it is a district within the city of
New Braunfels. While the living have come and gone, however,
the ghosts of former residents have nonetheless remained . . .
Located along the Guadalupe River at the northern edge of New

Braunfels, the once-independent community was founded in the 1850s by German farmer Ernst Gruene and his sons, who purchased 6,000 acres of surrounding farmland, which they planted with cotton.

Gruene—both pronounced and meaning "green," like the color—attracted two or three dozen sharecropper families and grew into a thriving commercial center. It was aided by its location along the stagecoach route between San Antonio and Austin at the point where it crossed the Guadalupe and, in the 1880s, by the establishment of the International–Great Northern Railroad line. Originally known as Goodwin Community, the town was eventually renamed for its most prominent family. By the early 20th century, Gruene was a significant cotton ginning and shipping center that had two freight rail stations. But the good times were not to last indefinitely. A marker titled "Gruene Cotton Gin" that was placed by the Texas Historical Commission in 1989 sums up the early history, economic basis, and namesake of the village—and the cause of its initial demise: "Built on the site of an earlier grist mill, the Gruene Cotton Gin was constructed in 1878 by H. D. Gruene," the marker reads. "Powered by the Guadalupe River, the gin was steam-operated and served to process the vast amounts of cotton grown in the area. The gin played an important part in the economic development of Gruene, a community dependent upon the cotton crop. The gin was destroyed in a 1922 fire, and only part of the boiler room remains. A new electric gin was built at another location and served the community until the cotton crop was lost to a boll weevil infestation in 1925."

The Great Depression followed hard on the heels of the weevils, a combination that was too much for Gruene, and all but one of its establishments—Gruene Hall—went out of business. Post–World War II highway construction bypassed the town, the path of Interstate 35 lying a mile and a half to the east, and within a few years it was almost completely deserted.

Gruene enjoyed a renaissance beginning in the 1970s, with the restoration of Gruene Hall, the old store, and a number of other local buildings, which culminated in the district being added to the National Register of Historic Places in 1975. Today, the bustling little community features a half-dozen restaurants, among them Adobe Verde and the sprawling Grist Mill, both established in old industrial structures; the Gruene Mansion Inn and Bed and Breakfast; about two dozen specialty stores of various sorts, making this a great place to hunt for gifts with local color; Gruene Hall, which today styles itself "the oldest dance hall in Texas" and which is famous throughout the state as a great venue for live music; and a couple of river rafting and tubing outfitters. Many of these businesses operate out of the village's original structures, most of which have some sort of ghost stories, if not actual hauntings, associated with them.

Adobe Verde, a "Tex-Mex cocina y cantina," is located in a historic electric cotton gin that dates to the 1920s. Paranormal phenomena people have reported at the restaurant include objects flying off of counters, lights turning on and off on their own, and the sound of booted feet running around the upstairs dining area when no one is there. Some people attribute these activities to a ghost of a man named Frank, believed to have been a groundskeeper who had his heart broken by the woman he loved and was moved to take his own life by hanging himself from the rafters of the factory. The tragic circumstances of his story notwithstanding, some hold that the spirit of Frank is responsible for this prankish behavior.

Another establishment in the village reputed to be haunted is the Gruene Mansion Inn bed and breakfast, a Victorian-style house that was constructed of timber-framed adobe in 1872 by Henry Gruene, second son of original settlers Ernst and Antoinette Gruene. Henry was distinguished for participating in the longest trail ride in U.S. history, a journey that took him all the way to Canada, and after he returned, around 1878, he purchased the family farm and all its buildings from his brother Ernst Jr.

This building, along with a number of adjacent ones once lived in by the Gruene family, are now believed to be haunted by the spirits of their former owners. Other structures believed to be inhabited by Gruene family ghosts include the oldest house in Gruene, located across the street and where Henry lived for a time until marrying and building the mansion; and the red-brick house next door to it, where he lived until selling the town and many other buildings to development company Rathgeber, West, and Leach in 1974.

There is also almost always something going on in Gruene. The historic town sponsors a variety of special events throughout the year, including many food- and music-oriented activities and Old Gruene Market Days the third weekend of every month except December and January. So stop by, visit it yourself—and, when you are there, ask the owner, bartender, server, or whoever is available to talk to at the places you are visiting about the ghost stories associated with them and what they might have personally seen or otherwise experienced.

CHAPTER 16

The Mansion
BOERNE/KENDALL COUNTY

SOMETIME AROUND 1870, a French architect named
Frank LaMotte constructed the impressive limestone building on Main Street in the town of Boerne that has since been
known in the local area simply as the Mansion. This tradition
is reflected in the name of the restaurant, La Mansion, that is

located in it today. And just as its name has been carried down
through the years, so too have the stories of spiritual activity in
the house and a persistent reputation for being haunted, even as
it has been passed to different owners and used for a variety of
purposes.

In 1872, the sumptuous home was purchased by a man
named Rudolph Carstanjen, who was probably an immigrant
from Germany or Bohemia and possibly an artist, among other
things, but about which little more is known. In 1883, a local
woman named Matilda E. Worcester purchased the home for
$2,800. Then, in the early 1900s, the ground floor of the build-
ing housed a drugstore, and its upper level was used as an annex
to the former Phillip Manor Hotel across the street. A woman
named Augusta Phillip bought the home in 1923 and owned it
for 20 years, living in it until she married a man named Henry
Graham (and possibly deciding to spend the afterlife there as
well, as we shall see). The Gilman Hall family purchased the
building in the early 1950s and lived in it themselves for about
two decades until, in the 1970s, it was converted into a restaurant, for which it has been used ever since.

Several people owned the Mansion over the following years
until a woman named Sue Martin purchased the building, completely remodeled it, and in 1984 reopened it as the Country
Spirit restaurant. She quickly came to believe that the home was
haunted and had this suspicion reinforced by others.

"Several psychics who have visited the place have told the
owner that the ghost should be referred to as 'David,' [who] seems
to prefer the upstairs men's restroom," Docia S. Williams says
in her book *Spirits of San Antonio and South Texas*. "David was a
local orphan boy in his early teens. Having no family, he took up
with the people who resided in the mansion, and the cook there
would often give him handouts from the kitchen. He was also
allowed to play with the children of the household. There was

a driveway, used for buggies then, at the side of the house, and that is where the children liked to play. David either fell or was pushed down on the driveway, most likely by accident. He sustained injuries from which he could not recover and soon died. This event is said to have taken place sometime in the 1890s."

While the events described in this often-retold story are not impossible, they do not ring true to me, and feel very much like the sort of thing I have seen psychics and mediums of limited ability contrive to fill in the gaps in their readings. My sense is that one or more ghosts almost certainly haunt the site and that one of them could very well be named David. But who dies from injuries sustained from falling down in a driveway? And why would that lead to the spirit of such a person becoming unquiet and remaining in its place of death? The fact that there is a historical record of the people who have owned and lived in the house make it all the more inexplicable that this story would fail to identify the family that supposedly cared for the mysterious orphan.

If there is any truth to the story at all it would actually be much more likely that, for whatever reasons, David was killed or that being an orphan he did not enjoy quite the hospitality of the household and consequently succumbed to abuse or neglect. Texans are also not particularly known for their generosity toward those who have suffered misfortune and an actual teen-aged David would have much more likely been expected to work for his scraps rather than receive them in exchange for playing in the driveway. In one variant on this story, David dies after being kicked in the head by a horse and if this is not actually any closer to the truth, it does at least sound more credible.

"A number of eerie events have been reported in the building," Robert Wlodarski, who revisited the site in the decade after Docia Williams did, says in his *Texas Guide to Haunted Restaurants, Taverns, and Inns.* "A candle was once seen moving from one side of a table to the other as stunned guests, who were having dinner, looked on in amazement. A middle-aged man, sitting at the bar in the rear portion of the building, watched in awe and fear as wine glasses suddenly flew off the shelves, one at a time, and smashed on the floor in front of him, narrowly missing his feet."

Some of the other phenomena that people have reported at least since the Mansion has been used as a restaurant are also suggestive of the presence of invisible hands. These include beer taps turning on by themselves, lights at the bar inexplicably turning off, spoons being flung across the kitchen by an unseen force, disembodied footsteps, and sounds of laughter and revelry from areas of the building where no one is present.

"Paranormal investigators also have encountered the spirit of Augusta Phillip Graham in the women's bathroom, usually as a reflection in the mirror that glares back for an instant before disappearing," Wlodarski continues in his book. "Graham has also been spotted standing in the ladies' room when women walk in. Upon entering, women often see an 'odd-looking' woman standing near the stalls and think nothing of it until the wraith suddenly vanishes as they take a second look."

Wlodarski reiterates the problematic story about the ghost known as David and also describes a ghost that has been dubbed Fred, who is reportedly seen sitting at a particular table and eating or simply watching people before disappearing. According to some sources, Fred lived in Boerne and died around the time the Mansion was built and can also sometimes be encountered in its cellar.

When my wife and I visited La Mansion and had lunch there in July 2014, we chatted with our waiter a bit about the restaurant and he confirmed that he and other staff have continued to experience phenomena of the sort described by the authors who had visited it in the decades before me. I then took the time to explore the building as much as I reasonably and circumspectly

could, paying special attention to the upper level, including a secondary dining area and the aforementioned men's restroom (and taking special care, as I always do when taking pictures in such areas, to not give the impression that I was not in any way interested in photographing the activities of living people).

For what it's worth, we also had an excellent lunch at the restaurant and were impressed with the menu, which had many traditional Mexican items that do not turn up at typical Tex-Mex restaurants. She had *sopa mercado,* a traditional type of chicken soup. I fell back on a taco platter, and we both enjoyed the three kinds of homemade salsa that came with our complimentary corn chips.

La Mansion certainly bears visiting by anyone interested in the paranormal, whether they would like to conduct a formal investigation or just have a meal in a place where spirits are firmly believed by many to be present. As I have found in any number of places I have visited and written about over the years, whether the stories about them are true actually has very little to do with whether or not they are really haunted.

CHAPTER 17

Ye Kendall Inn

BOERNE/KENDALL COUNTY

ONE OF THE MOST IMPRESSIVE and welcoming of
the many haunted establishments that can be found throughout
Hill Country is, without a doubt, Ye Kendall Inn, the sprawling
hotel, restaurant, and event complex that dominates the main
square in the town of Boerne.

Ye Kendall Inn is well known in the local area for being
haunted, and I was well aware of its reputation before visiting
it for the first time. I was therefore both amused and took it as
an auspicious sign that, when I walked into the hotel bar, the

barmaid and a patron were discussing the odds that some items that had ended up on the floor in the kitchen had been flung there by a ghost. My wife and I were also struck by the irony that some of the patrons in the bar at that point were having a few drinks ahead of a wake that was about to start there for a local man who had recently died. Perhaps his spirit will join those that have long been noted in this historic hostelry that has its roots in the mid-19th century and the early days of settlement in the rugged hills northwest of San Antonio.

On April 23, 1859, Erastus and Sarah Reed purchased a 5.2-acre plot of land along the banks of Cibolo Creek, the stream around which Boerne was established, for $200. Upon this site they built a substantial Southern Colonial home that featured a long front porch and 22-inch-thick walls constructed with heavy, hand-cut blocks of limestone quarried from the surrounding hills. (Today this structure forms the middle section of the inn.) It included a cellar and a secret tunnel that could be used to escape the building in the event it was attacked by any of the hostile Comanche or Apache Indians that still wandered through the surrounding wildlands.

Following the custom of the era, the Reeds rented out rooms in their home to travelers and people staying in the area for a short time, foreshadowing its ultimate role as an inn. This use of the property was expanded when it was leased in the following years by a man named Harry W. Chipman, who rented rooms to stagecoach passengers. He also allowed local ranchers, who kept their cattle penned in what is now the municipal park preparatory to moving them up the Chisholm Trail to stockyards in Kansas, to store their wagons in the area now occupied by the Limestone Grille Restaurant.

A succession of people subsequently purchased the home and either dwelled in it or used it for commercial purposes.

In 1869, politician, lawyer, and newspaperman Henry B. King moved to Boerne and purchased the property, and he left his wife Jean to manage the household whenever he rode to Austin to serve in the state senate.

Nine years later, in 1878, Dallas businessmen C. J. Rountree and W. L. Wadsworth bought the property and began operating it as the Boerne Hotel. They also significantly expanded the original home, adding a large wing at each end of the building so that it could accommodate more guests.

Then, in 1882, an English couple named Edmund and Selena King purchased the Boerne Hotel. On September 26 of that year, however, Edmund was tragically killed in a hunting accident behind the inn (quite possibly giving us a name to associate with one of the spirits that apparently haunts the property today).

Throughout the 1880s, the hotel served as a stagecoach inn, providing travelers with a place to rest and drivers with the opportunity to swap out horses. During that era it was purchased by a Dr. H. D. Barnitz, who renamed the establishment Ye Kendall Inn in honor of journalist and pioneer George Wilkins Kendall, the man for whom the county was named.

Robert L. and Maude M. Hickman acquired the hotel in 1922 and owned it for more than two decades, until 1943, and during their tenure they greatly modernized the establishment and added many private bathrooms to it.

In 1982, Ed and Vicki Schleyer acquired Ye Kendall Inn and took significant steps toward restoring and upgrading it, adding hardwood floors, new mantels to the fireplaces, and other improvements that contributed to its appearance and comfort. They also learned only after taking possession of the property that it was widely believed to be haunted—something they themselves came to believe when they began to experience all sorts of strange phenomena in their new home. These included hearing heavy disembodied footsteps coming from parts of the

building where no one was present; the sound of doors opening and then slamming shut even when they were securely locked; crystal prisms falling off of chandeliers; doorknobs rattling; and the building's electricity failing to work for no apparent reason. One area in particular, the Marcella Booth guest room, has reportedly been the site of a number of odd events and accidents.

"In the 1980s, while the place was being restored, a worker fell through the floor as he tried to install a bathroom fixture," Docia S. Williams writes in her *Spirits of San Antonio and South Texas*. "The claw legs kept falling off of an old bathtub. Strange things just kept happening in that same room for no apparent reason." The covering on the bed is also often indented, as if someone has been sitting on it, even when no one has been in the room since it was last tidied up.

The Schleyers were not the only people who experienced paranormal phenomena at the inn, and one profound episode involved a guest who encountered a spectral woman in Victorian-era garb who identified herself as Sarah. Could this have been the shade of Sarah Reed, who, with her husband Erastus, first built upon the property more than a century earlier?

In addition to the main building of the inn there are also more than a dozen historical cottages and cabins, and even a small church that has been turned into a suite, available for overnight guests. These have been relocated to Ye Kendall Inn from around the state of Texas and add whole new dimensions of history and paranormal possibilities to the property.

With such a colorful history and so many people passing through its doors, dwelling in its rooms, and experiencing the full range of human emotions within its walls, it is perhaps not surprising that Ye Kendall Inn would have a reputation for being haunted and have so much ghostly lore associated with it. That being the case, I was almost surprised that no anomalies turned up in any of my photos or audio recordings and that I did not experience anything that might be interpreted as supernatural in origin.

I was not, however, disappointed, because it is not reasonable to expect spirits to perform on demand or reveal their presence during the short piece of eternity that a living person is visiting their haunt. And I did very much enjoy the ambience, history, and hospitality of the place during the few hours that I spent exploring its halls, public areas, and guestrooms, and left looking forward to my next visit and a more detailed investigation of Ye Kendall Inn.

Austin

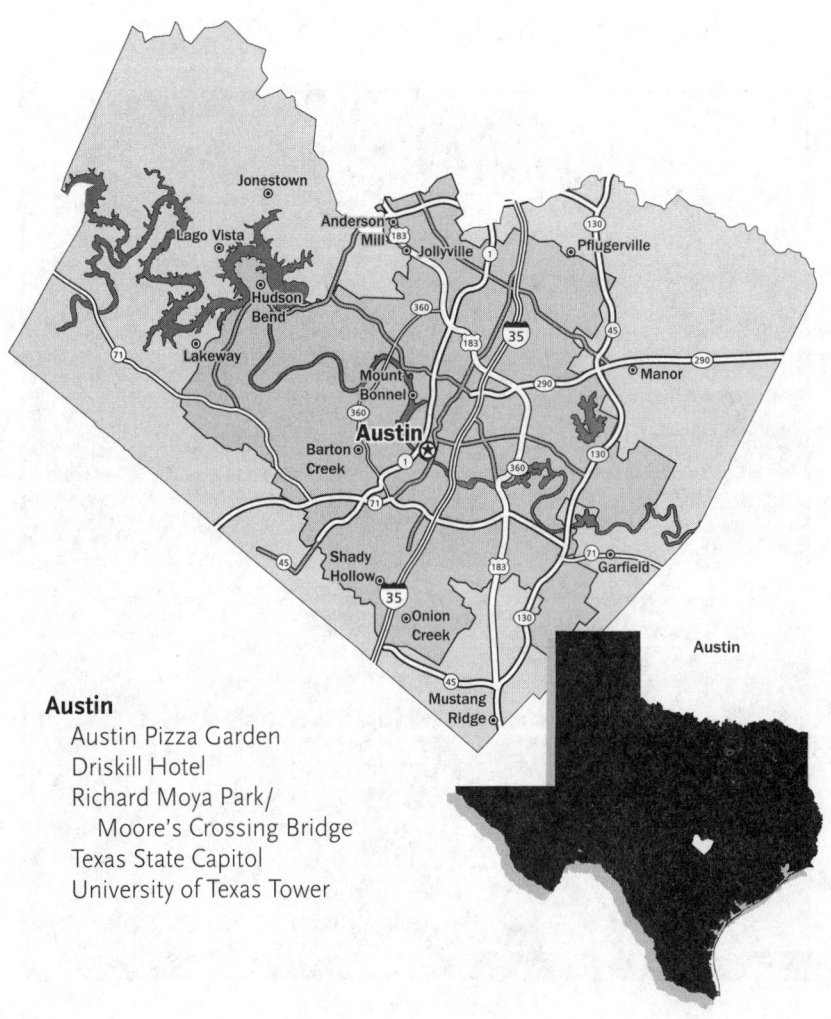

Austin
  Austin Pizza Garden
  Driskill Hotel
  Richard Moya Park/
    Moore's Crossing Bridge
  Texas State Capitol
  University of Texas Tower

CHAPTER 18

Austin Pizza Garden
OAK HILL/SOUTHWEST AUSTIN

SUFFICE IT TO SAY, when I was scouting reputedly haunted locations in Austin I was immediately skeptical that something characterized as a pizza restaurant was likely to be inhabited by ghosts of any sort and expected it would not appear in this book.

When I learned, however, that Austin Pizza Garden is located in a building more than a century old, my interest was piqued, and after I visited it, I was sold on its merits as both an eatery and object of paranormal investigation.

One of the first things I saw on the limestone-block structure when I ventured out to it was the Texas Historic Landmark marker from 1970 that established its provenance and stated its original name: "OLD ROCK STORE. Influenced by the style of early German rock buildings in central Texas, James Andrew Patton (1853–1944) supervised the construction of this building in 1898. A German mason laid the stone. Patton fought Comanches as a Texas Ranger and was a civic leader and local postmaster. He was known affectionately as 'the mayor of Oak Hill.' He and his family, followed by others, operated a general store here for many years. The building also housed a local Woodmen of the World lodge on the second floor."

A stone set into the wall of the building, in fact, has an even earlier date on it, 1879, along with the engraved initials J.A.P., tribute to an even earlier structure that Patton had constructed on the site (squarely in the era of the vicious Indian Wars that wracked Texas in the late 19th century). Patton and his wife, Virginia Catherine Bishop, ran the store and raised a family that included their two children, Andrew Lewis Patton and Rosa Selma Patton, and their nieces, Beulah, Lillian, Zelda, and Cora White.

Rosa later inherited her father's shop and married Texas Ranger John Dudley White, who in 1918 was killed in the line of duty in Broadus, Texas. After spending much of her life running the store, Rosa left it to her daughter Margaret White Grunewald, who later turned the building over to her nephew James White (co-owner of the Broken Spoke, a legendary southwest Austin honky-tonk).

What is now known as Oak Hill was initially called Live Oak Springs and was a colorful area. In 1835, the Mexican government awarded the land to William Cannon, as part of its attempt

to attract settlers from the United States with an eye to strength-
ening the area against Indian attacks and aiding its development. In 1865, Confederate partisans attempted unsuccessfully
to have the community renamed Shiloh after the Civil War Battle of the same name. Four years later, however, it was changed
to Oatmanville, and in 1870 a post office named Oak Hill was
opened, although it would be some time before this name was
adopted for the area over all.

In the years that followed the War Between the States, Oak
Hill's woodlands of live oak and juniper—the latter referred to colloquially in the local area as "mountain cedar"—attracted settlers,
particularly ones from Appalachia eager to help meet the national
demand for lumber. Conflicts broke out among area woodcutters,
contributing to Oak Hill's rough-and-tumble reputation. Hides,
wool, cotton, and pecans were other staples of the local economy.

By the early 1880s, Oak Hill was home to about 75 residents and consisted largely of a general store and four saloons.
It enjoyed a boom when stone quarried in the areas around it
was used to build the Texas State Capitol in downtown Austin,
which also spurred construction of the Austin and Oatmanville
Railway, used to ship limestone from the community to the city
(and which, its purpose fulfilled, was abandoned in 1888). Oak
Hill grew slowly over the following century; it had somewhat
more than 200 residents by 1904 and only around 400 by the
1970s. Its growth then spiked in the 1990s, shooting up to more
than 11,000 as it became a suburb of Austin, and in 2000 it was
absorbed by the city.

My wife and I visited Austin Pizza Garden midafternoon on a
weekday in February 2013, between the lunch and dinner rushes,
which made it an ideal time for our purposes. We spoke with one
of the managers. While we ate one of the restaurant's delicious
Cajun shrimp pizzas along with a couple of glasses of wine, he let
us read through a binder containing the detailed but inconclusive

results of an investigation of the site by a local ghosthunting group. We then took some time to explore and photograph the interior of the building with special attention to areas where paranormal phenomena of various sorts has been reported, particularly the kitchen and a back stairway leading from it to the second level. We also chatted with a number of staff members about things they have experienced at the restaurant and learned about some of the many legends and events associated with it.

Jayme Garza, who has worked at the restaurant for nearly two decades, has experienced a number of things at it. Some years back, for example, while she was washing dishes in the kitchen, she says that she glanced up the nearby stairs and saw a figure in white looking back down at her. She also said that when she is in the meeting room on the second floor she sometimes has the feeling that someone is walking around behind her, but when she looks, no one is ever there.

Innumerable other employees of the restaurant have reported strange events of various sorts as well. These include hearing disembodied footsteps (sometimes more than one set of them),

seeing lights going on and off on their own, noticing doors opening on their own, finding items lying on the floor after leaving a
room and coming back to it—and, on rare occasions, even seeing items flung across the room! Perhaps not surprisingly, many
have also experienced a sense of disquiet, especially at night or
when by themselves.

Customers also sometimes claim to experience things of
various sorts at the restaurant. Foremost among these are people
who are psychically sensitive and who sometimes say they can
feel invisible presences around them.

Other stories about the building the restaurant is located
in describe spectral faces appearing on the walls and then
fading away.

Theories vary widely as to whom the resident ghosts might
be, how many of them there are, and why they are apparently
so active at the restaurant, but Patton and his kin are among
the most likely candidates. Author Jeanine Plumer, founder of
Austin Ghost Tours, and Monica Ballard, one of her guides, have
investigated the site and come to the conclusion that it is haunted
by the spirit of slain ranger John Dudley White, who returned
in death to be with his wife. Age and continuous habitation of a
site are among the most common factors accounting for haunting, and the vibrant and multicultural history of the area only
enhances these possibilities. Over the years, the building also
has served as a post office, art gallery, and more.

We did not experience anything of a paranormal nature during our visit to Austin Pizza Garden, but that, of course, is too
much to take for granted, even at a place that all indicators would
suggest is haunted. We did, however, enjoy a good meal, have
the opportunity to investigate the site to the extent we wanted,
and heard some compelling stories about things people have
witnessed there. And, if you visit, that is probably the least you
can expect as well.

CHAPTER 19

Driskill Hotel
DOWNTOWN AUSTIN

THERE ARE MANY REASONS to recommend the Driskill Hotel and any number of things that might make it appealing to visitors. It is the oldest operating hotel in the state capital of Texas, is steeped in history, has any number of colorful stories associated with it, and is beautiful and luxurious. As one might expect from its inclusion here, of course, it is also widely reputed to be haunted, and the hotel does nothing to discourage this belief.

When my wife and I visited the hotel and had brunch in its 1886 Cafe and Bakery one Sunday in November 2014, I asked our waiter if the property was haunted, and he immediately responded that he believed it was. He then also went and got us a couple of handouts provided by the hotel, one that listed some of the hauntings associated with it and another that described its mundane history.

In 1849, Tennesseean Jesse L. Driskill emigrated to Texas; eight years later he became a cattleman, and when the Civil War broke out, he sold livestock to the Confederate States of America and received from it the honorary title of colonel. He initially made a fortune as a war profiteer, but, as a result of backing the losing side, eventually lost it. In 1869, however, he moved to Austin and became a wealthy cattle baron, businessman, and community leader by the 1880s.

Driskill decided that he wanted to build a grand hotel that would rival those in cities like New York, Chicago, St. Louis, and San Francisco, so in 1884 he bought the lot at the corner of Brazos and what is now Sixth Street for $7,500.

"One of the finest hotels in the whole country," according to the *Daily Statesman* newspaper, opened in December 1886. Well, it should have been recognized as such, in that it cost Driskill $400,000, the equivalent of about $94 million today! The massive building took up half a city block. It was to have a tumultuous history, to be bought and sold many times; to be closed at various points; to be periodically expanded, renovated, and modernized; and to serve as a venue where politicos and other affluent and influential people met, stayed, and conducted their affairs. With the hopes and dreams, schemes successful and foiled, and negative and positive emotions of thousands of people who have spent time at the Driskill—and the few who might have died there—it is perhaps not surprising that the hotel would have acquired a reputation for being haunted.

Driskill's ambitious plans had an auspicious start: On New Year's Day 1887, the hotel hosted the inaugural ball for newly elected Governor of Texas Sul Ross. This tradition was ultimately reprised by a number of other Texas governors, including William P. Hobby (1917–1921), Miriam "Ma" Ferguson (1925–1927), Dan Moody (1927–1931), John Connally (1963–1969), and Ann Richards (1991–1995). But in the short term, Driskill had to contend with some significant issues.

To start with, the Driskill was considerably more pricey than most other local hotels in what was still, in many respects, a frontier capital—charging $2.50 to $5 a night, as compared to the more typical 50¢ to $1—which limited the number of people willing or able to stay at it.

Then, in May 1887, about six months after the hotel opened, half its staff—including its general manager, head waiter, and main bartender—were hired away by the Beach Hotel in Galveston, a calamity that forced the Driskill to shut down until they could be replaced.

By October of that year, Driskill had hired new key personnel and managed to reopen his luxury hotel. A much larger disaster that the colonel would not be able to recover from, however, was looming.

During the winter of 1887–88, a severe drought combined with extreme cold killed off much of the Driskill cattle herd, destroying the family fortune. According to legend, the colonel tried to recoup his wealth by gambling what he had left but instead ended up losing the hotel to his brother-in-law, Jim "Doc" Day, in a high-stakes poker game. Driskill succumbed to a stroke within two years, the fruits of his life's work taken from him and his dreams unfulfilled.

Day capitalized on his new acquisition by hosting lavish events for dignitaries from throughout the United States and abroad when Texas dedicated its new pink granite capitol building in May 1888 (see Chapter 21). Five years later, however, Day traded the hotel for a ranch and vineyard in California, plus $14,000 in cash.

The following year, the hotel was sold twice to groups of investors. Then, in 1895, cattle baron, banker, and Texas Ranger George R. Littlefield purchased the hotel for $106,000 and went on to invest an additional $60,000 into improvements to it. These included electric lighting, steam heating, bathtubs in 28 rooms, electric fans in every room, frescoes on the ceilings, and a bank in the lobby. Littlefield kept the hotel for eight years and then sold it at a loss to a man named Edward Seeling.

In 1909, a ladies' hairdressing salon and Turkish bath opened in the storefront facing Sixth Street. In response to this, psychic healers and medicine men selling elixirs were drawn to the hotel and ushered in an era of spiritualism at it.

A new round of expansions and renovations was implemented in the early 1930s, including the addition of a 13-story tower and conversion of the original 60 guest rooms to include private bathrooms. More significant from the point of view of paranormal investigators was the creation of the Maximillian Room. This striking chamber takes its name from the eight famous gold leaf–framed mirrors once owned by Emperor Maximillian of Mexico, each of which bears the image of his wife, Empress Carlota, reputed to be one of the most beautiful women in the world. These artifacts had somehow ended up in a San Antonio antique shop but in 1930 were discovered and purchased by the Driskill. These mirrors are arranged so that they create an infinite cascade of reflections of each other and anything reflected in them. Some of those who have visited this room, however, have reported being stunned to spot individual spectral figures looking back at them from within the depths of the reflected images!

That is just one example of the numerous ghosts that are widely believed to haunt the Driskill today. Foremost among these, unsurprisingly, is Colonel Driskill himself. Four months after he died, the hotel commissioned a portrait of him that now hangs above the landing on the grand staircase in the lobby, and his ongoing spiritual presence in the hotel seems to radiate from it. He is noted for causing the smell of cigar smoke to manifest in guest rooms and for making the lights in their bathrooms go on and off by themselves.

Guests also periodically claim to be awakened by the sensation of someone pushing them out of bed or that the furniture in their rooms is moved while they were asleep. People also have noticed some of the elevators running on their own or the cars stopping and their doors opening on floors that no one has selected. It is unclear, however, whether the colonel or some other resident specters are responsible for these and other inexplicable little episodes. Hotel management has identified a number of them and notes that "they are both helpful and mischievous."

"According to Driskill lore, a U.S. senator was visiting Austin and stayed at the hotel," a list of hauntings compiled by the hotel says. "While he was attending an event on the mezzanine, the senator's 4-year-old daughter was playing with a ball near the grand staircase. The young girl tripped and fell to the base of the stairs, tragically dying. Some nights, she can be heard bouncing the ball down the steps and giggling."

Another one of the ghosts that has been identified in the hotel is a woman named Mrs. Bridges, who worked at the front desk for several years in the early 1900s. She did not die at the Driskill but apparently had an emotional connection to it, because her shade, dressed in the Victorian-style uniform that female employees of that era would have worn, can sometimes be seen there at night. Those who claim to have spotted her say they have seen her moving out to the middle of the lobby, where the old front desk used to be located, fussing over the flower arrangements that would have been displayed there.

"Peter J. Lawless lived in the hotel from 1886 until 1916," the Driskill's record of hauntings continues. "Though the hotel closed several times during this period, Mr. Lawless stayed on, often without staff. He had a key to his room as well as the key to the front door. Sometimes when the elevator doors of the fifth-floor Traditional Wing open, Mr. Lawless can be seen checking his pocket watch."

There are also a number of tales that are somewhat grimmer in tone that the hotel does not include in its official history, but it is unclear whether they are true or not anyway.

One of these urban legends involves a woman who supposedly shot herself in the abdomen, possibly in room 429 sometime in the 1990s, and then bled out in the bathtub. Her blood-drenched spirit is believed by some to haunt the room in which she ostensibly died. According to some accounts, she wanders the halls of the floor on which it is located.

Another story describes two "suicide brides" who, left standing alone at the altar on the days of their weddings, took their own lives in a particular room of the hotel, possibly 525, 10 years apart. Like the other story, however, there are no names associated with this account and apparently no official records to support it.

Whether they are substantiated by records or not, there are ample stories of paranormal activity associated with the Driskill Hotel and probably a better-than-usual chance of encountering something supernatural there. Even if you do not, however, you will at the very least enjoy a visit to one of the most enduring and historic hospitality venues in the Lone Star State.

"Ghost of a Texas Ladies' Man"

Austin may be the first city of Texas, but it also styles itself "the live music capital of the world." Many musicians have consequently stayed at the Driskill while in Austin for the festivals and other events held there, and, like anyone else, some of them claim to have experienced paranormal phenomena at the hotel.

Singer Annie Lennox is among those who have stayed at the Driskill while performing in Austin. "Undecided about what to wear to the concert, she laid out two dresses before taking a shower," the Driskill says in the list of hauntings it has compiled. "When she got out of the shower, one of the dresses had been put away."

While numerous people have experienced paranormal phenomena at the Driskill, one in particular, Johnette Napolitano, lead singer for the alternative rock band Concrete Blonde, commemorated her profound supernatural experiences there in the 1992 song "Ghost of a Texas Ladies' Man":

I saw a face in the shower door
A cowboy smiled, came and faded
I reached for my towel on the floor
I didn't think it was exactly where I laid it
"You don't scare me, you don't scare me," I said
To whatever it was floating in the air above my bed
He knew that I would understand
He was the ghost of a Texas ladies' man
I reached to turn out the light
He wouldn't let me get near it
He seemed so glad to see a woman in the flesh
And I really liked his spirit
"You don't scare me, you don't scare me," I cried
To my ectoplasmic lover from the other side
He knew that I would understand

He was the ghost of a Texas ladies' man
"You don't scare me, you don't scare me," I cried
To my ectoplasmic lover from the other side
He knew that I would understand
He was the ghost of a Texas ladies' man

CHAPTER 20

Richard Moya Park/Moore's Crossing Bridge

SOUTHWEST AUSTIN

To those uninterested in or oblivious to the PARANORMAL, Richard Moya Park, a wooded tract of land along the banks of Onion Creek, is best known for its bridge, which consists of three black-iron spans that were once located in downtown Austin. Initially constructed at a cost of $45,000, it served as a toll bridge for just two and a half years, until June 18, 1886, when it was closed and then removed to make way for a wider span. The history of the bridge is briefly described on a Texas Historic Landmark marker erected at its south end in 1980: "MOORE'S CROSSING BRIDGE: This structure was originally part of a six-span bridge across the Colorado River at Congress Avenue in Austin. Constructed there in 1884, it was designed by the King Iron Bridge and Manufacturing Co. of Cleveland, Ohio. In 1910 it was dismantled and placed in storage. Five years later three spans were rebuilt here but destroyed the same year in a flood. The current bridge, comprised of the remaining spans, was completed in 1922."

What the marker does not say is that the bridge itself is believed by many to be haunted and has been the subject of numerous ghostly tales over the past century, most of which allude to an ill-fated romance that ended in violent death. Many visitors to this Blackland Prairie site, especially those who have actually walked across the bridge, have also reported seeing apparitions of various sorts. For what it is worth, the site in Austin where the bridge used to be located has no accounts of paranormal phenomena whatsoever associated with it as far as I am able to ascertain. (It is, however, noted for being home to about 250,000 bats, which perform one of the most impressive twilight emergences in the country.)

One of the most common phantasms people claim to witness at the site is a ghostly man and woman in outdated clothing, sometimes hand-in-hand, walking across the bridge. Some people also say they have seen a lone man in archaic clothing waving to them from the bridge but that when they try to get a closer look at him he disappears.

Another apparition people see at the bridge is the specter of a man hanging from a tree, the apparent victim of a lynching, in some cases with a ghostly and grief-stricken woman looking up at him. In some of these accounts the hanged man is described as black and is sometimes said to have been killed by vigilantes because of his interest in, reciprocated or otherwise, a white woman.

This is actually a fairly common type of story that can be found at many ostensibly haunted sites throughout the country, particularly in the South, and I have personally encountered it in several states. There is a much less common variant that is sometimes told in conjunction with this site, however, that describes a white man who is killed because of his involvement with a black woman. Whether his killers were a white mob, the outraged relatives of the woman, or something else altogether, however, is not clear. And, as is typical in the case of such stories, there do not appear to be any official records to substantiate any such events at or around this site.

Some people also claim to hear the hanged man speak and to utter phrases that have included "I didn't do it" (presumably before the noose tightened around his throat and prevented him from saying anything at all).

Prior to construction of Moore's Crossing Bridge, people who wanted to cross Onion Creek in this area had to use the low water point located here. This was frequently problematic, however, because this stream, which rises about 70 miles to the west in the Hill Country near Johnson City and then flows into the nearby Colorado River, is prone to overflowing its banks after any sort of rain. The flood that destroyed the bridge in the early 1900s was not, in fact, an isolated incident, and this continues to be an issue in the area. In October 2013, for example, there was such heavy flooding and the park was so badly damaged that it was closed for more than six months, reopening only during the following summer. When I visited the park after a rain in November 2014, much of it was once again flooded and at least one building that had been wrecked more than a year earlier was still unrepaired and unused.

Moore's Crossing Bridge is no longer open to automobile traffic and has been replaced for these purposes by a much more innocuous concrete span that crosses over the stream on Burleson Road, off which Richard Moya Park is located. The old iron bridge is open to foot traffic from within the park, however, and during daylight hours people can freely ascend it via a footpath at its northern end and walk across it to the far side of Onion Creek. It was bright and sunny the day I did this, conditions ideal for taking pictures but perhaps less likely to encourage manifestations of paranormal phenomena. From atop the span I obtained a good view of the swiftly flowing creek, the temporary ponds that had been formed among the groves of big oak and pecan trees growing throughout the park, and the handful of Hispanic families walking along the path, picnicking, and gathering nuts.

When I reached the other side of the bridge, I discovered the aforementioned historical marker and could see that the footpath continued and bore out of sight to the left. Following this led me onto Moore's Bridge Road, a paved but rutted and unmaintained track that runs parallel to Burlseon Road and is connected to it by FM 973, which it runs into after a short distance; a little farther south I could see the artificial upland of the Travis County Landfill.

While the park is closed after dark, I realized, anyone who wanted to conduct a nighttime investigation of the bridge could easily drive down this road as far as a pair of flanking concrete blocks, beyond which it would be difficult to turn around. They could then continue on foot to within sight of the bridge and—as the park appears to be located wholly on the north side of Onion Creek—could presumably conduct an investigation without falling afoul of any laws or authorities as long as they did not actually venture onto or across it.

And, I reflected, perhaps that is exactly what I will do next time I visit Moore's Crossing Bridge.

CHAPTER 21

Texas State Capitol
DOWNTOWN AUSTIN

FEW, IF ANY, PLACES IN A PARTICULAR STATE
are cauldrons of so many conflicting passions, beliefs, and moti-
vations as their capitol buildings, and there is not one that has
not over the years acquired a reputation for being haunted. It

should thus hardly be surprising that the capitol of a state that has historically been so marked by violence, corruption, and zealous ideologies as Texas should have a wealth of ghostly lore and strange phenomena associated with it.

"The capitol is haunted day and night," Fiona Broome, a psychic, ghosthunter, and author of *The Ghosts of Austin, Texas,* said in a 2008 interview. "If you've got a nice, misty day there, people see ghosts walking up the path to the capitol building all the time."

Designed in 1881 and completed in 1888, the Texas Capitol is located in downtown Austin and contains the office of the governor and the offices and chambers of the state legislature. It is the fourth building to serve as the state capitol, the one immediately preceding it having burned down in the great capitol fire of 1881. It has a footprint of 2.25 acres and some 360,000 square feet of floor space (more than any other state capitol building), nearly 400 rooms, more than 900 windows, and, at 308 feet in height, is the sixth-tallest state capitol (and one of several taller than the U.S. Capitol in Washington, D.C.).

Construction of the Italian Renaissance Revival–style structure was funded by an 1876 article of the state constitution that authorized the sale of public lands for the purpose. In one of the largest barter transactions in recorded history, capitol builders John V. Farwell and Charles B. Farwell, known as the "Capitol Syndicate," were paid with more than 3 million acres of public land in the Panhandle region of Texas (a tract that served as the XIT Ranch, one the largest cattle ranches in the world, from 1885 to 1912).

Cornerstone for the structure was laid on March 2, 1885—Texas Independence Day—and the completed statehouse was opened to the public on April 21, 1888—San Jacinto Day. It was constructed largely by migrant workers and convicts, as many as a thousand at any given time, and value of the land combined with other expenses contributed to a total cost of $3.7 million for the original building.

Originally the plan was to construct the building entirely of limestone from the community now known as Oak Hill, located about 10 miles away to the southwest. After the limestone started to become discolored, however, it was found to have a high iron content. When they learned of this problem, the owners of Granite Mountain—a solid dome of pink granite at nearby Marble Falls—offered to donate to the state, free of charge, however much sunset-red granite it would need to complete the project. Thus, while the statehouse is fashioned largely of Oak Hill limestone, most of it is hidden behind its outer walls and within its foundations. This red granite was subsequently used for many other state government buildings throughout the Austin area.

In the 13 decades since it was completed, the Texas statehouse has been renovated and expanded a number of times, in response to everything from damage to the building to a need for more space. One of the first big modifications was implemented in 1955, with the addition of central air-conditioning.

On February 6, 1983, a fire broke out in the chambers of Lieutenant Governor William P. Hobby Jr. A policeman and four firemen were injured, and a 23-year-old man was killed in a fierce blaze that came close to destroying the statehouse and severely damaged its east wing and cast-iron framing. Restoration of the severely damaged building took 10 years, and the state took advantage of the need for extensive repairs to modernize mechanical and structural systems. Texas also sought to address the growing lack of space in the old building and decided to add a new office wing. The best place for an addition was the plaza directly to the north of the capitol, but this would have eliminated the building's historic facade and covered a traditionally important public space, so the state decided to have the new area built below rather than above ground. In 1993, the four-story subterranean Capitol Extension was completed, doubling the square footage of the complex and providing many improvements; despite its great size, there is little evidence of this expansion at ground level beyond the four-story open-air inverted rotunda and numerous skylights camou-flaged as rows of planters.

Two years later, in 1995, a comprehensive interior and exterior restoration of the original building was completed. Finally, in 1997, the 22 acres of parklike grounds surrounding the capitol were renovated and restored.

Exploration of the capitol, its grounds, and its history reveals any number of individuals, events, and incidents that tie in with the ghosts and supernatural lore associated with the site.

Any number of factors make it easy to believe that the rotunda, centerpiece of the capitol, might indeed be haunted, starting with the fact that it is a whispering gallery in which even quiet utterances in one part of it can be heard in others. This circular area features paintings of every president of the Republic of Texas or governor of the state of Texas, and the south foyer also features a large portrait of David Crockett, a painting showing the surrender of General Santa Anna at the Battle of San Jacinto, and sculptures of Stephen F. Austin and Sam Houston. Whether this area is haunted by any of these personages is not clear, but it is easy to feel their presence within it.

The rotunda is believed to be haunted by the ghosts of workers killed during construction of the capitol. One of the guides I spoke with at the Texas Capitol Visitors Center, a young woman named Annie, told me that one worker in particular is said to have plummeted from the top of the dome while working on it. According to this legend, she said, he smashed fatally onto the floor of the rotunda some 300 feet below, and any number of people passing through this area alone or late at night claim to spot his shade in it.

Another legend Annie told me about holds that the capitol is haunted by the ghosts of women who were members of the Daughters of the Confederacy. Embittered by the misfortunes of the South during the War Between the States and the indignities suffered by it afterward, their unquiet spirits are among those believed to continue to roam the halls of the capitol building.

Some 17 monuments surround the Texas Capitol, many of which flank a tree-lined Great Walk of black-and-white diamond-patterned pavement, and they evoke the spirits of those whose actions and sacrifices they commemorate. First among these honors the Heroes of the Alamo, installed in 1891 as part of an effort to improve the appearance of the grounds, and it was followed soon after by ones dedicated to volunteer firemen, Confederate soldiers, and Terry's Texas Rangers. More recently, the Texas Capitol Vietnam Veterans Monument was dedicated on March 29, 2014.

When I visited the Texas Capitol in April 2014, I had the opportunity to chat with Byron, one of the official guides who does ghost tours of the capitol, both around Halloween and upon request by visiting groups.

"A couple of years ago, we had someone who worked for the lieutenant governor who saw what he thought was a woman in 1940s dress walking down the hall behind the Senate chamber," Byron told me. "She turned a corner and he thought she went into a room, but when he caught up to the spot where she disappeared it seemed as if she had actually gone through a wall."

The employee naturally thought this was strange, Byron said, but did not dwell upon it too much. Sometime later, however, in the course of his duties he went into the lieutenant governor's reception room—an area behind the Senate chamber that used to be the lieutenant governor's apartments but which has been turned into a sort of meeting room/ballroom—and saw a picture of her hanging there!

"It was the wife of governor Coke R. Stevenson," Byron said. "He was governor in the 1940s here in Texas, and his wife, Fay Wright Stevenson, passed away from cancer in 1942, while he was in office." Those who have encountered this ghost, however, say she seems friendly and not frightening in any way.

Another ghost people claim to encounter over the years in the Texas Capitol is that of Comptroller Robert Marshall Love, who was shot and killed by a disgruntled associate in his first-floor office in 1903. He has allegedly startled state troopers and tourists alike when they have spotted him walking up the promenade toward the building, clad in a period business suit and sometimes a top hat.

Yet another specter many people claim to have seen over the years is that of an unnamed "Lady in Red," who is often encountered on the third floor near a stairwell and the offices once occupied by House Speaker Pete Laney. This has led some to conclude that the mysterious woman might have been the illicit lover of Laney or someone on his staff who, spurned in life, continues to haunt the building in death.

Many witnesses have also have seen mysterious handprints that appear on foggy mornings in the condensation of a senate reception room window in the capitol's east wing, despite repeated cleanings. Some believe they are left by the ghost of the young man who died in the 1983 fire.

"People tend to be skittish at night, and their imagination probably works on them," state historian Bill Green, who served from 1986 to 1989, said in a 2008 interview of the many accounts of supernatural events he heard during his tenure in the Texas Capitol. Then he added, indicating how his experiences in the building may have affected him personally, "I do believe in ghosts."

CHAPTER 22

University of Texas Tower
DOWNTOWN AUSTIN

VISITORS TO THE MAIN BUILDING CLOCK tower on
the University of Texas (UT) campus in Austin who know nothing
of its history might well wonder why it has security on par with
that of a regional airport. People wishing to enter the tower must
do so as part of an organized tour and are cautioned that after
doing so they cannot leave before it is over. The hallway leading
to the tower elevators is guarded by two armed police officers and
a metal detector, and before going through it, purses, backpacks,
and the like must be checked with tour staff. When visitors exit
the elevator on the 27th floor they will see yet another policeman,
and when they walk up to the 30th floor and the observation deck,
they will discover yet another one on duty there. The open areas of
the observation deck itself are completely enclosed in metal cag-
ing with spaces just wide enough to slip a camera through. What
is perhaps just as interesting as these stringent measures is that
absolutely no reference to them is made at any point during the
50-minute tour. They are based, however, on terrible events that
occurred at the 307-foot-tall tower since its completion in 1937.
These events, and possibly the spirits of the disturbed individuals
who perpetrated them, haunt the UT campus to this day.

On August 1, 1966, 25-year-old Charles Joseph Whitman, a
former marine and an architectural engineering student at the
university, launched a bloody rampage that left 18 people dead
and 42 wounded by the time it was over. Whitman's bloody campus attack was the worst in U.S. history up to that point (and was
not eclipsed until April 2007 when a student went on a killing
spree at the Virginia Tech campus in Blacksburg, Virginia).

Exactly what caused Whitman to snap when and in the way
he did is not entirely clear, but it probably had a lot to do with the
brain tumor that was discovered in the autopsy following his death.
Severe headaches, amphetamine abuse, and a dysfunctional family life probably all played their role as well. Whitman's father had
been a demanding, authoritarian perfectionist who was known

to be both physically and emotionally abusive to the members of his family. The situation escalated in early 1966 when Whitman's mother left his father and, with Whitman's assistance, relocated from their home in Lake Worth, Florida, to Austin, Texas (a move that prompted his father to begin calling him several times a week to implore him to convince his mother to return to Florida). The dissolution of the family and the strains associated with it was, in fact, the primary subject of a discussion Whitman had with a psychiatrist six months before his attack.

Whitman also was troubled by a number of failings that were indicative of emotional instability. These included receiving a court martial in 1962 for gambling, threatening another marine, and keeping a personal firearm on base; loss of a scholarship to the University of Texas in 1963 for butchering a deer in his dorm room; and striking his wife, Kathy, on a number of occasions. It also bears mentioning, however, that Whitman had become an Eagle Scout at the almost-unheard-of age of 12, scored highly on IQ tests, and was honorably discharged from the U.S. Marine Corps after a relatively uneventful enlistment.

By the summer of 1966, Whitman had hopped through at least four jobs since being discharged from the Marine Corps 20 months earlier, had visited five doctors and a psychiatrist over the previous year, and was doing poorly in school. He had reached his breaking point.

Shortly after midnight on August 1, Whitman went to his mother's house in Austin and killed her with a hunting knife he had bought just the day before (along with binoculars and some Spam). He then returned to his own home and stabbed his wife three times in the heart with the same weapon.

"I imagine it appears that I brutally killed both of my loved ones," he wrote in a note right afterward. "I was only trying to do a quick thorough job . . . If my life insurance policy is valid, please pay off my debts . . . donate the rest anonymously to a mental health foundation. Maybe research can prevent further tragedies of this type.

"I talked with a doctor once for about two hours and tried to convey to him my fears that I felt [some] overwhelming violent impulses," Whitman continued later in the note. "After one visit, I never saw the doctor again, and since then have been fighting my mental turmoil alone, and seemingly to no avail."

Whitman then proceeded to load his service footlocker and a wooden crate with a sawed-off shotgun, a bolt-action hunting rifle equipped with a scope, an M-1 carbine, and a .35-caliber pump rifle; 12 boxes of ammunition and numerous clips, magazines, and loose rounds; and various other pieces of equipment, including food, camping gear, and a machete, three knives, and a hatchet. On his person, he carried three pistols, including a .357 magnum revolver, a 9mm automatic, and a 6.35mm automatic. Whitman had been fascinated with firearms since childhood and had been trained to use them by his father. His experience as a hunter and a marine helped him to master his shooting skills.

Transporting his arsenal on a handcart he had rented for this purpose, Whitman went to the UT campus, about 3 miles from his home, and proceeded to the university's tower, where he took the elevator to the 27th floor. He then painstakingly hauled the weapon-laden handcart up the stairs to the observation deck. And then all hell broke loose.

Whitman started by butt-stroking the receptionist on duty with one of his rifles, knocking her unconscious (and causing her to die a week later). He then barricaded the stairway and, when a group of people tried to get past it, fired into them with his shotgun, killing two and severely injuring two more.

At that point, at 11:48 a.m., Whitman began firing with his sniper rifle at people on and around the campus below. Even people who heard the gunfire did not understand what was going on, and several students were shot dead before anyone even called the police.

Once the situation was understood, every on-duty police officer in the city was dispatched to the campus, where they were joined by off-duty officers, troopers from the Texas Department of Public Safety, deputies from the Travis County Sheriff's Office, and a number of armed civilians. This assemblage began firing up at Whitman's position.

Impeded by the fire from below, Whitman was forced to take cover and to use the waterspouts at each corner of the tower as gun ports, severely limiting both his visibility and opportunity for targets.

As the firefight continued, the authorities called in a spotter plane with a sniper of their own, and it began circling the tower while the rifleman onboard traded shots with Whitman. Turbulence made it difficult for the airborne police officer to get a good shot at the killer, and return fire from the tower struck the aircraft, driving it back to a safe distance, where it continued to circle until the incident was resolved.

Three police officers and a civilian stormed the tower and made it onto the observation deck, where they caught Whitman by surprise and engaged him at close quarters. One officer fired six shots from his .38 revolver at Whitman, and another discharged his shotgun at him twice, killing him. Almost inexplicably, the other officer then grabbed the shotgun from his companion, rushed up to Whitman, and shot him again.

Ninety-six minutes after it began, the shooting spree was brought to an end. On the campus mall and Guadalupe Street below, dozens of people lay dead, dying, or injured. After the incident, officials closed the observation deck to the public for two years, reopening it in 1968.

While Whitman's bloody rampage was the most lethal and dramatic of the incidents associated with the tower since it was completed in 1937, it was by no means the only one.

"Death was part of the tower story before the building was even finished," Charles Beach wrote in a 1999 *Austin American-Statesman* article. "Construction worker Charles Tanner slipped on a scaffolding and fell to his death in 1935 . . . . Alton Parker Thomason taught English and had an office on the 24th floor. On Monday, June 11, 1945, he went to his office . . . locked the door and opened the window, took off his shoes and socks, slashed his throat, forearms and left ankle with a razor blade, and jumped . . . . Edward Graydon Grounds was next, on Saturday, October 15, 1949. The 19-year-old student from Dallas hit the roof of the main building. He left a notebook on a banister of the observation deck that contained . . . notes on a classroom test on the velocity of objects dropped from high places. About 8:45 [on Friday, May 12, 1950], several witnesses saw a woman sitting on the ledge of a window between the 26th and 27th floors. Then she was hanging by her hands and seemed to be trying to pull herself back inside. [Bennie Utence Sellers] dropped, falling 3 feet from a university employee who was picking up scraps of paper off the ground . . . . On Saturday, March 3, [1951, Harry Julius Rosenstein] jumped from a window and slammed into a parapet on the roof 11 floors down."

Suicides resumed after Whitman's attack when on May 4, 1971, William Dunlap flung himself from the observation deck of the tower. On September 29, 1971, an emotionally disturbed Ruth Moment Armistead ended her own life by jumping from the edifice. On December 1, 1973, Warren Lee Ogburn did so. And when Lenard Bruce Kreuz Jr. used the tower as a gateway to the afterlife on October 27, 1974, university leaders decided to close it indefinitely, and it remained off limits for the following 25 years.

Then, in 1999, school officials decided to once again allow the public to visit the observation deck of the tower, albeit under very strict conditions (although it was closed for more than two years following the terrorist attacks of September 11, 2001, and did not reopen until 2004).

Nothing about the tragic history of the tower is even vaguely alluded to during the carefully managed tours, and information is mostly limited to the physical characteristics of the structure and debunking amusing rumors about the structure few people are even aware of and that are supposedly spread by other educational institutions. When I asked our student guide about the Tower Garden, however—which contains a plaque "dedicated to the memory of all those who died and those whose lives were touched by the August 1, 1966 shooting"—she denied such a thing even existed! This assertion is all the more inexplicable in that the university periodically uses the garden for ceremonies to commemorate the deaths in the previous year of people affiliated with its community. Whether her denial was a matter of policy or personal initiative is unclear, but it certainly made her claim to know "everything" about the tower somewhat questionable, or at least irrelevant.

Suffice it to say that ghost stories are not among the anecdotes about the UT Tower that the cautious guides tell. Many people, however, have felt strange and disturbing but unseen presences and experienced other paranormal phenomena in and around the tower and the adjacent memorial garden and sensed the veracity of Beach's contention that "certain spots seem to call out to the despondent, the depressed, the psychotic." The building has consequently acquired a justifiable reputation for being haunted, both by the troubled spirits of those who climbed the tower so that they could do violence to themselves or others and those who fell prey to them or other misfortune.

My wife and I visited the tower most recently on a bright and sunny day in November 2014 and conducted as much of an investigation of the site as we could, given the constraints in place. Other than a profound feeling of melancholy in the indoor portion of the upper level, however, I cannot say that we experienced anything that we could definitely say was paranormal in character; nothing irregular showed up in any of our photographs and even if we had captured any voices with our digital recorder, they likely would have been muffled by the winds that whip the observation deck of the tower. But do not be surprised if you visit the tower and sense a troubled presence, or obtain evidence suggesting that the tormented ghosts of Whitman or one of the other people who breathed their last here might yet haunt the halls and stairways of this ivory tower of death.

Texas Hill Country

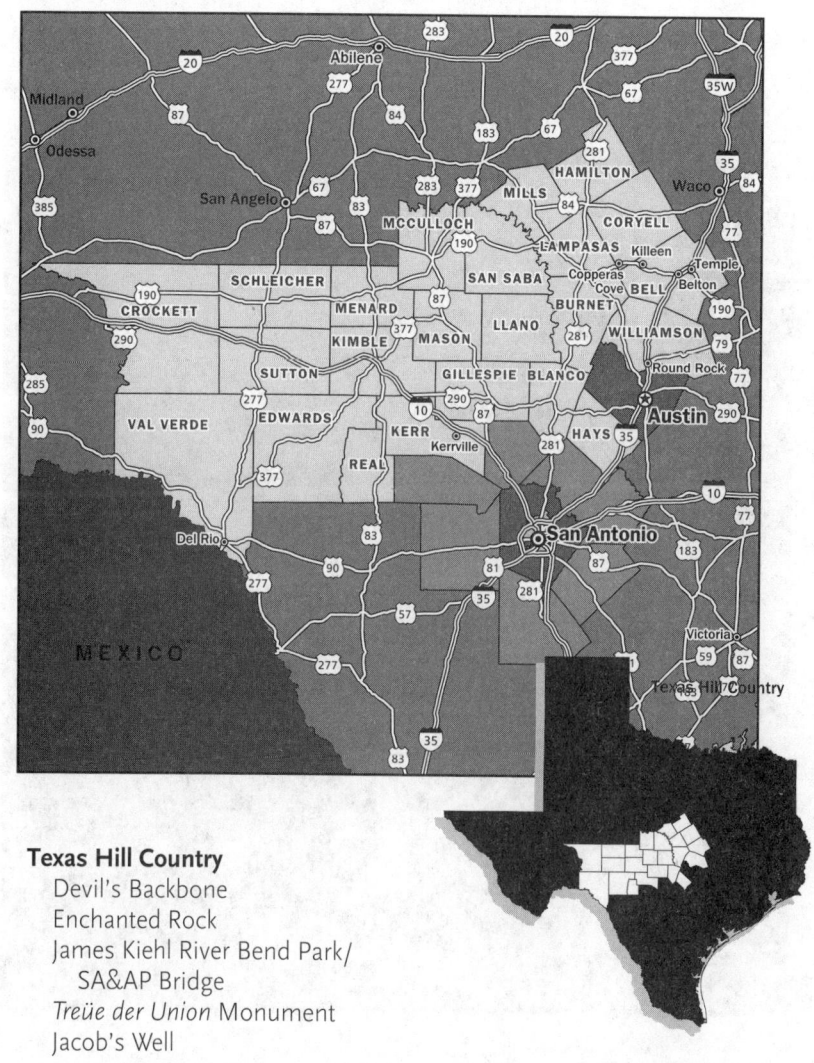

Texas Hill Country

153

CHAPTER 23

Devil's Backbone
BLANCO COUNTY/COMAL COUNTY/ HAYS COUNTY

ONE OF THE FIRST PLACES I explored after moving to Texas Hill Country was the Devil's Backbone, a haunted high-way that runs along a rugged ridgeline corresponding to Farm-to-Market Road 32. Since then I have driven along it many times,

154

conducted investigations at a number of sites on it, and even taught at a haunted historic school located on it, and it does not seem much less strange to me than it did initially. Parts of this road seem mysterious and haunted under the best of conditions, and it is little wonder that it should have ghostly lore associated with it.

The Devil's Backbone is about 23 miles long and most of it runs along the northern edge of Comal County. Its western end, however, is anchored in Blanco County, where it intersects with Highway 281, and its eastern end lies in Hays County, just south of the village of Wimberley and at the intersection with Ranch Road 12. Having a name at all in a state where a disproportionate number of roads are known only by numbers is distinction enough, to be sure, and having a name straight out of a Western is at least twice as good.

That Western ambience is not just a coincidence, of course, and cowboys once ran cattle along the Devil's Backbone and enjoyed the same striking views that reward travelers to this day. Sections of this drive are, indeed, very beautiful, and at several places travelers can see the land descend dramatically from the edge of the escarpment and then rise up into rolling hills to the north. This drive also will be very enlightening for anyone who might have wondered why irregular Comal County is shaped the way it is; the diagonal, northeastern boundary of the county runs parallel to the Devil's Backbone and, following the topography of the region, essentially has one of its edges formed by it.

FM 32 is a strange little stretch of road that somehow feels more isolated than it should and that is almost Gothic in its features. Ancient farmsteads lay in the woods and fields along its length, some clearly occupied, some obviously abandoned, and others apparently somewhere in between. Old model trucks, some perfectly preserved and others rusting away, sit in yards and meadows. Twisting lanes, a few with appropriately eerie names like Purgatory Road, lead off to the north and south, their mysteries concealed almost immediately behind wooded bends.

Lone hunters and hikers exploring the trails that wind along the slopes of the Devil's Backbone have reported seeing the apparitions of Indians following closely behind them. Some local residents also claim to have seen ghostly cattle ranchers driving their herds through the hills or the ghosts of Spanish monks or conquistadores. Yet others have told of spotting phantasmal troops of Confederate cavalrymen and hearing the sounds of pounding hooves outside their homes but afterward found no evidence that any horses were actually present. And while exploring one of the dry creek beds that descends from the ridgeline, a haunted ravine known as the Devil's Hollow, I have, among other things, inexplicably heard the sound of a bell chiming just beside me but with no visible source.

I conducted my most recent investigation of the Devil's Backbone starting the evening of Thursday, March 28, 2013, and continuing into the morning of Good Friday, March 29, 2013—and was welcomed by an orb that turned up in my very first photo, at the western end of the highway!

Bolstered by such an auspicious start, I continued eastward from there and made my first stop at a bump in the road known as Green's Hollow. It is located on the banks of the Little Blanco River, which is straight as an arrow at some points, flanked by immense cypresses, and—usually completely dry—looks more like some long abandoned road than any sort of waterway. Some of the numerous memorials devoted to those who have perished on the Devil's Backbone are located here, about 6 miles from the intersection with Highway 281 and one of three locations along the road convenient for those interested in conducting investigations of it. I spent some time there, examining the area and shooting a series of photos, and then continued on down the dark and deserted road.

After another 5 miles or so, I reached the historic hamlet of Fischer, located about halfway along the Devil's Backbone and another of the convenient places to stop along the road (and incidentally, just 6 miles from my home). Its main features are the historic Fischer Cemetery, a post office, and the original family Fischer store itself, which has operated off and on at the site for more than a century and a half. Today, the long, corrugated metal building is both a museum and an antique shop run by Charlene Fischer, whose great-grandfather opened the original general store on the site in 1853. (The current structure was built in 1902.)

"There were cattle drives through here," Charlene said of her ancestors' decision to establish a store on the Devil's Backbone during my first visit to her store in 2009. "It took so much land to run cattle that everyone was very spread out and it was a fairly large trade area at the time." Because of this, she told me, the store had two large warehouses for storing inventory, one of which still stands today.

No one was around during my March 2013 nighttime stop in Fischer, as has been the case every time I have visited the hamlet after dark, and after taking a few obligatory shots of the familiar landmarks, I resumed my journey.

Continuing on another 8 miles or so, I reached a picnic area, the third location on the haunted highway that is a convenient place for visitors to stop. During the day, this is an especially good place to take a break and enjoy a dramatically sweeping view of the Hill Country, but little can be seen at night beyond a number of homemade shrines, some dating back to at least 1991, that have been established here. Presumably, most of the people commemorated at this spot died elsewhere along the highway and are memorialized in the rest area because of the ease of visiting and maintaining memorials in it.

After conducting my business at the picnic area, I continued on another 4 miles to the eastern end of the Devil's Backbone. Then, my adventure for the night concluded, I made my way back home to download my photos and see if any former travelers along the haunted highway and I had crossed paths with each other.

Back in the old days, driving the Devil's Backbone was very tough, Charlene Fischer told me, and Model Ts had to run up the steepest slopes backward because they were not powerful enough to go up them forward without overheating. It is a somewhat easier drive today, of course—and, at the very least, a bit of an excursion into the haunted history of Comal County.

CHAPTER 24

Enchanted Rock

GILLESPIE COUNTY/LLANO COUNTY

FOR AS LONG AS ANYONE CAN REMEMBER, and perhaps even longer, Enchanted Rock has been a special place, from the earliest human inhabitants of the region, as much as 12 millennia ago, right up to the people who visit it today. Native Americans believed it was a portal to the other-world, and there are countless legends, ghost stories, and para-normal phenomena associated with this wondrous natural site, whose name is not arbitrary or just meant to be colorful.

Enchanted Rock is an almost unbelievably massive pink granite pluton formation called a monadnock that is located in the Llano Uplift south of the Llano River, about 15 miles north of Fredericksburg, and the state natural area in which it is located spans Gillespie and Llano Counties. The rock itself covers approximately 640 acres and rises about 425 feet above the surrounding landscape to an elevation of 1,825 feet above sea level. It is the largest formation of its sort in the United States. Approaching visitors are often stunned to see the huge pink dome rising up from the surrounding countryside, and it is visible for miles around. Huge as it appears to be, however, Enchanted Rock is just the visible above-ground portion of a large igneous batholith that formed some 6 million years ago and was subsequently exposed by erosion of the surrounding sedimentary rock, primarily limestone.

More than 400 archeological sites on or around Enchanted Rock indicate that people inhabited the area as far back as 12,000 years ago, and, equipped with flint tools, weapons, and fire, these Paleo-Indians formed the basis of what would develop into Plains Indian culture.

Famous conquistador and explorer Álvar Núñez Cabeza de Vaca was probably the first European to lay eyes upon Enchanted Rock, when he passed through the area in 1536. Tonkawa Indians inhabited the region at that time and told of how at night ghost fires glimmered at the top of the dome and how they could hear unearthly groaning noises emanating from it. Geologists have since attributed these noises to nighttime contractions of the rock after it has been heated by the sun during the day, but they led native peoples to dub it "Crying Rock" and "Spirit Song Rock."

Spaniards made efforts to settle the area in the 1700s, launched raids against the Lipan Apache, built a presidio and mission on the nearby San Saba River, and attempted to establish a silver mine on Honey Creek, near the Llano River. They were never able to completely control the area, however, and in 1821 the colonial power was ousted during the Mexican War of

Independence. Just 15 years later, Mexico itself lost its hold on it as well, when revolutionaries seized control of the entire region and founded the independent Republic of Texas in 1836.

In 1838, Texan couple Anavato and Maria Martinez were granted ownership of the land containing Enchanted Rock, and in 1841, Texas veteran and politician James Robinson acquired the property. That year, legendary Texas Ranger Captain "Jack" Hays was surveying land in the area when a band of Indians attacked him and his companions. Cut off from the others, Hays fled up to the summit of the rock and took shelter in a depression there. For three hours, he held off his assailants until his companions were able to assist him. This episode is commemorated on a historical marker at the site that reads:

"From its summit in 1841, Captain John C. Hays, while surrounded by Comanche Indians who cut him off from his ranging company, repulsed the whole band and inflicted upon them such heavy losses that they fled."

In 1844, Robinson sold the land containing the rock to lawyer, politician, and signer of the Texas Declaration of Independence Samuel Maverick, who had it surveyed for minerals. Enchanted Rock then changed hands at least four times between 1881 and 1927, when rancher Tate Moss inherited it and opened it as a tourist attraction. In 1936, during the centennial of Texas independence, the site was made a Texas Historic Landmark, and over the next decade or so the land changed hands a few more times.

Then, in 1970, the federal government declared that Enchanted Rock was a National Natural Landmark. Owners Charles H. and Ruth Moss decided to sell the property in 1978 and initially approached the Texas Parks and Wildlife Department, which was unable to afford their asking price. On March 1 of that year, at the behest of Lady Bird Johnson, the Nature Conservancy, a charitable environmental organization, acquired the property for $1.3 million and agreed to act as interim owner until the state of Texas could take over, thereby ensuring that the area would not be subjected to private development. Soon after that, the U.S. Department of the Interior announced it would make available a federal land and water conservation grant that Texas could use to purchase the area as soon as it was able to match it with state funds. In October 1978, Enchanted Rock State Natural Area was opened to the public. By 1984, facilities were installed and it was added to the National Register of Historic Places.

Tonkawa, Apache, and Comanche Indian folklore all attribute magical and spiritual powers to the rock. While attempting to hide from settlers, local Indians would take refuge on the top two levels of the dome, where they could not be seen by people on the ground below, and this may have been prompted by or created the belief that anyone spending the night on the rock would become invisible. There was also a widespread belief that misfortune or even death would befall anyone who ascended the rock with ill intent, as well befits a sacred site.

It is hard to tell if other stories originated with Indians, even though they are about them, and after a point, much of the folklore associated with the area is a product of its increasingly composite culture. Settlement by Spaniards, Mexicans, Texans, and Americans all led to the addition of more stories about strange occurrences around Enchanted Rock, including accounts of human sacrifices being made upon it by Comanches and Tonkawas. Perhaps related to this is the explanation of footprintlike indentations on the rock as those of an Indian chief who sacrificed his daughter and whose spirit is now said to be condemned to walk the rock eternally. And in a twist on this theme is the possibly factual account of Spanish soldier Don Jesús Navarro's rescue of a friendly chief's daughter after she was kidnapped by Comanches intending to sacrifice her on the rock.

One of the most lurid and complex stories associated with the site is about a Spanish priest who, being chased by Indians, fled to the rock, disappeared into it, and eventually returned with a tale of falling into a cavern and wandering through a labyrinth. During his odyssey, he reportedly encountered many spirits before finally escaping after two days beneath the surface of the earth.

And, just as gold must figure in stories of the conquistadores as much as glory and God, Enchanted Rock was believed by some to be the location of a silver mine or the hiding place of the lost treasure of El Dorado.

Ghost stories, of course, figure prominently in the wealth of lore related to Enchanted Rock. One legend holds that the spirits of a now-extinct tribe slaughtered by rivals haunt the slopes of the great rock, and another that the daughter of an important chief flung herself off the dome and to her death after seeing her people killed (and, maybe, somewhere in the murky past, these two stories have the same root and a basis in fact). Another says that "screams" that can be heard at night are those of a white woman who hid on the rock after escaping from the Indians who had abducted her.

Enchanted Rock is at the center of an incredibly rich natural area as well. More than 500 species of plants, from four key plant communities—floodplain, granite rock, mesquite grassland, and open oak woodland—can be found on or around it. (Texas Hill Country overall is, in fact, one of the most ecologically diverse areas on the planet and is home to a stunning 1 *percent* of the world's terrestrial plant species.)

Enchanted Rock is also home to a variety of fauna, including bats, foxes, ring-tailed cats, squirrels, the Texas horned lizard, and perhaps most surprisingly—within seasonal vernal pools, ecologically fragile depressions located at the crown of the rock—fairy shrimp. Numerous species of birds also can be found around the rock, including finches, flycatchers, grosbeaks, hummingbirds, jays, roadrunners, sparrows, vireos, wild turkeys, woodpeckers, and many varieties of difficult-to-tell-apart birds that many naturalists waggishly lump together as LBJs (little brown jobs).

Activities in the park also go beyond paranormal investigation and include caving, primitive camping, rock climbing, picnicking, and hiking. When I visited Enchanted Rock for the first time in April 2014, it was, in fact, for some of those more mundane activities and with a group of more than 20 children, which limited me to a fairly rudimentary ghost hunt. Climbing up to the top of the dome on the popular Summit Trail, however, gave me a sense for the magnificence of the site and why so many people have attributed spiritual properties to it.

We also had the opportunity to clamber a little ways down the far side of the summit to a relatively unobtrusive opening in the boulders that was conveniently labeled CAVE ENTRANCE.

Unable to resist and being armed with a flashlight, I ordered the kids to not follow me and headed in.

For about the first hundred feet or so I did not even really need the light because there were ample gaps in the tumbled boulders to allow the rough passageway to be illuminated by the bright Hill Country daylight. The tunnel then more or less ended in a sheltered area surrounded by rocks and vegetation but open to the sky, and, at the right side of it, a hole descended into a dark, natural chamber below.

One of the parents in our group told me he had continued into this cave and that it took 20 or 30 minutes to pass through and opened up farther down the far side of the rock. I could not leave my group for the time it would have taken to make that passage and then climb back up the hill, so I decided to defer this particular excursion until my next visit to Enchanted Rock. Looking down into the depths, however, I recalled the story of the Spanish cleric who had spent two days within the hill, and wondered how many little passageways did or used to exist—among them ones that might not have looked promising to anyone but a person desperately trying to hide from pursuing Indians but then opened up into other areas.

A visit to Enchanted Rock is certain to be a rewarding experience for anyone interested in the natural or the supernatural worlds. And, if you are lucky, you might just cross paths with the spirit of one of the many Indians, explorers, or settlers who have visited this magnificent site and left some of themselves at it.

CHAPTER 25

James Kiehl River Bend Park/ SA&AP Railway Bridge

COMFORT/KENDALL COUNTY

TO THE HISTORY OF A STATE that has long experienced violence as one of its hallmarks have been added America's most recent wars in Iraq, Afghanistan, and the areas surrounding them. One reminder of this on the outskirts of the village of Comfort in Kendall County is James Kiehl River Bend Park, dedicated to a local soldier killed in these ongoing conflicts. A stone installed in 2008 by the Kendall Country Partnership for

Parks in the pleasant, 25-acre recreational area along the banks of the Guadalupe River is inscribed with these words: "This monument is placed in honor of Army Spc. James M. Kiehl and of the men and women of Kendall County who have served and are serving in the Armed Forces of the United States of America. We salute you and thank you. May this stand as a remembrance of your sacrifices and efforts in defending our country and maintaining our freedom."

A resident of Comfort, Kiehl joined the U.S. Army and underwent basic and advanced training at Fort Jackson, South Carolina, and Fort Gordon, Georgia. He was thereafter assigned to the 507th Maintenance Company in Fort Bliss, Texas, near El Paso, where he was tasked with repairing computers and fiber-optic cable. Then, on February 17, 2003, Kiehl's unit was deployed to the Middle East in support of the 31st Air Defense Artillery Regiment in what would become the 2003–2011 Iraq War. A little more than a month later, on March 23, the 507th was at the tail end of a larger formation that was part of the U.S. advance on Baghdad and accidentally went the wrong way at a road junction, into the town of Nasiriyah. Ambushed by Iraqi government forces, the company lost nine of its members in the ensuing firefight, among them Kiehl. Five were wounded and six were captured. (One of those captured was Private First Class Jessica Lynch, subject of a famous rescue by U.S. Special Operations Forces the following month.)

Kiehl's remains were returned to Comfort and laid to rest there on April 2 in a ceremony that included full military honors. He was survived by his wife and a son who was born two months after he was killed.

Anyone conducting an investigation in or right around James Kiehl River Bend Park may very well record any of the anomalies typically associated with reputedly haunted places, such as orbs, inexplicable mists, or even EVPs. They are not likely, however, to get much of a sense for whether they are detecting the spiritual presence of Paleo-Indians, Apaches, Comanches, conquistadores, settlers, the shingle-makers who camped nearby, or soldiers from the 19th or 21st centuries. There are also at least four small cemeteries dating at least as far back as the 1800s in the vicinity of the park. It is the old railroad bridge a short distance from the recreational area, however, that most ghosthunters will intuitively be drawn to.

It would be hard to do much online research about haunted sites in the San Antonio area without stumbling across references to a site dubbed "Tro Bridge." It is typically identified as being somewhere in Bexar County, the county where San Antonio is located, but most sources do not bother to give its specific location, just that it is "a long bridge that is above water." At least one paranormal research group, however, Alamo Haunts, makes the case that it is located instead in adjacent Kendall County and is, in fact, the bridge over the Guadalupe River just a short distance from James Kiehl River Bend Park. Paranormal phenomena associated with the Tro Bridge reputedly include the sensation of hands grabbing at the legs of anyone attempting to cross it and a subsequent sense of panic that inevitably keeps people from making it all the way across.

The bridge near James Kiehl River Bend Park is a massive, three-truss span that is sometimes referred to as the Guadalupe River Railroad Crossing. It has been measured at 1,070 feet in length—somewhat longer than three football fields—and has had its metal tracks removed and is now surfaced only with rotting wooden ties. It was built by the former San Antonio and Aransas Pass Railway (SA&AP Ry), which existed from 1886 to 1925, and was on a now-discontinued branch that ran from San Antonio northwest into Kerrville via Comfort, more or less following the current route of Interstate 10 between those points. Anyone driving by on nearby Ranch to Market Road 473, the main east-west

road that runs through Comfort and the most convenient approach
to the park, can hardly avoid being struck by the appearance of the
rusted iron bridge some 0.6 mile to the south. I am probably not
the only person who initially assumed that the park must have
been located at the site of the bridge and was surprised to discover
that it was actually another 0.7 mile down the road.

The area around the bridge itself is surrounded by fences
and marked with signs prohibiting entry, so attempts to cross
the bridge or even directly examine its infrastructure would
involve trespassing. We naturally decided to forego doing so during our visit to the site—any temptations I might have had to
the contrary being suppressed by the presence of my wife and
parents. It is a very old bridge and not in very good shape, so the
risk of injury can be added to supernatural and legal hazards for
anyone attempting to cross it.

Alamo Haunts describes how its members did make a nighttime crossing of the bridge and how they had to crawl along
the last stretch of it to avoid being spotted by law enforcement
officers driving by. Their "amazing experience" was made creep-
ier by the sounds of hooting owls and the bleating sheep and
goats in the groves and fields around the bridge. According to
their account, they twice spotted a spectral black figure and did
indeed feel as if something were trying to pull them over the
edge of the bridge. They concluded that the site was definitely
haunted and that it was indeed the legendary "Tro Bridge."

There was reportedly a wreck at the site when an earlier version of the bridge collapsed under the weight of a freight train
many years before, killing a number of crew members, so that
could certainly account for it being haunted. It is possible to park
alongside the road at any number of points, however, and to get
unobstructed views of the bridge and its supports, so an investigation that did not involve actually walking across it would certainly be viable.

There is also a 1.5-mile-long trail at James Kiehl River Bend Park, the Pecan Loop, that follows the old rail bed for about 500 feet and might thus bear incorporating into an investigation of the area. Regardless of what else you might find, it is an enjoyable walk through woodland, grassland, and riparian zones and through stands of pecan, mesquite, cedar elms, and majestic bald cypresses rising up from the banks of the Guadalupe River.

CHAPTER 26

Treüe der Union Monument
COMFORT/KENDALL COUNTY

ONE OF THE STRANGEST, BLOODIEST, and most heartbreaking episodes in the saga of a violent state took place during the Civil War and has been known since among most people as the Nueces Massacre (a dissenting minority of people who applaud or are indifferent to this tragedy somewhat disingenuously refer to it instead as the Battle of the Nueces). A memorial to this terrible event, known as the *Treüe der Union* or "Loyalty to the Union" monument, can be found in the historic Hill Country village of Comfort. There is every reason to think it might be haunted by the spirits of those whose deaths it commemorates and whose remains it marks.

Beginning in the 1840s, thousands of German immigrants left their homeland for Texas, fleeing repressive government and limited economic opportunities and seeking to make a new life for themselves and their families. Many of them settled in or near the Hill Country, founding such towns as New Braunfels in Comal County, Fredericksburg in Gillespie County, and Comfort in Kendall County.

When people in Texas began contemplating secession from the union in 1860, on the eve of what would become the U.S. Civil War, a majority of the German immigrants were opposed to this for any number of reasons. Most were adamantly loyal to their new country, and many—being intellectuals, liberals, and people who benefited from the fruits of their own labors—were also opposed to the institution of slavery. This was all the more prevalent in Comfort, which was founded in 1854 by Freethinkers, members of an intellectual and a religious movement who established communities during this era in several parts of the United States, albeit most of them in the North. It is thus not surprising that a number of the Hill Country counties in which many of the Germans and Freethinkers lived—including Bexar, Gillespie, Kendall, Kerr, and Medina—voted against secession.

Revisionist histories about the universal desire of Southerners to do battle with the Yankee oppressors notwithstanding, the Confederacy could not induce nearly enough men to take up arms in its cause—slave owners generally being unwilling to and exempt from doing so—and its states had to institute drafts early on in the conflict. When Texas followed suit in the spring of 1862, its German citizens were among those who objected. Confederate military authorities responded by imposing martial law on central Texas and ordered all males age 16 or older to take an oath of allegiance to the Confederacy or leave the state. Many refused to take the oath. In retaliation for this, local thugs and military forces burned their farms and homes and lynched as many as 150 of them.

Seeking to avoid being either murdered or conscripted into fighting for a cause they were morally opposed to, some German settlers attempted to flee across the border into Mexico. In early August 1862, a group of 61 German Texans from the Hill Country, many from around the town of Comfort, left their families and headed for Mexico, guided by a militia recruiting officer named Jacob Kuechler and led by a Major Fritz Tegener. Most were conscientious objectors and a number of them were members of a civil defense organization that had been organized to protect against Indian raids and Confederate depredations.

By August 9, the Germans had covered about 150 miles and were encamped on the west bank of the Nueces River, in Kinney County, about 30 miles from the border with Mexico. They had been pursued, however, by a force of 94 Confederate cavalrymen under a Lieutenant C. D. McRae, which included members of an irregular marauder unit called Duff's Partisan Rangers. In the early-morning darkness of August 10, the Confederate horsemen attacked the German camp, which was not well guarded or established in a strong defensive position. Caught off guard, some 34 of the Germans were killed and nine of them badly wounded in the ensuing skirmish; two of the rebel troopers were slain and 18 of them injured, among them McRae. In the aftermath of the battle, the Confederate troops rounded up the nine wounded German prisoners and summarily executed them.

Eighteen of the Germans, including Kuechler, managed to escape during the battle. About half of them managed to make it back home; eight were killed two months later on the banks of the Rio Grande River while once again trying to cross into Mexico; and a handful ended up for a time in Mexico, California, or Union-held New Orleans. If any of them had any doubts about their aversion to the Southern cause, these had been thoroughly dispelled. Horrified by the brutality of the massacre, about 2,000 Union sympathizers abandoned their homes and fled farther into Hill Country.

After the war ended, Eduard Degener—father of two of the victims of the massacre, Eduard Steves and William Heuermann—paid $20 for a lot in Comfort for purposes of creating a memorial there. Remains of the Germans killed on the banks of the Nueces and Rio Grande were brought back to the lot in Comfort and interred in a mass grave there, except for those who drowned in the Rio Grande and could not be recovered. On August 20, 1865, some 300 people attended the funeral for them, which included a eulogy by Degener and an honor guard of Federal troops who fired a salute over the grave.

A year later, on August 10, 1866, on the four-year anniversary of the Nueces Massacre, a 35,700-pound obelisk inscribed with the words *Treüe der Union*— "Loyalty to the Union"—was dedicated. Built through donations by families of the victims and other local residents, the monument stands 20 feet high and was constructed of native limestone by local stonemasons and carvers.

This is the only German-language monument to the Union in the South where the remains of those killed in battle are buried, the only federal monument on former Confederate soil, and one of only a half-dozen burial sites where a U.S flag—an 1866 version with 36 stars, representing the number of states at the time it was dedicated—flies at half-staff in perpetuity, as ordered by Congress in 1991 during the 125th anniversary commemoration. It was designated a Recorded Texas Historic Landmark in 1968 and added to the National Register of Historic Places listings in 1978. In 1994, the Comfort Heritage Foundation oversaw a restoration conducted by stonemason Karl H. Kuhn from nearby Boerne.

Something that surprised me when I visited the *Treüe der Union* monument for the first time in April of 2011 was my discovery that a number of small stones had been carefully placed along the edge of the obelisk. This is, in fact, a sign of devotion practiced at Jewish cemeteries, and I was not familiar with any other religions that happened to do the same!

Did Comfort have a Jewish subcommunity, or were there Jews among the Freethinkers who founded it and settled in the surrounding area. Could some of the victims of the Nueces Massacre have been Jewish? There was certainly no mention of that in anything I read about the incident that mentioned Jews, and none of my subsequent research revealed anything.

The presence of these carefully placed little stones, however, struck me. Ashkenazi names are frequently indistinguishable from other German names, and any number of the victims of the massacre or resident families of the area could certainly have been Jewish. Jews were among the groups prompted to flee the repressive European governments of the mid-19th century; some might certainly have decided not to advertise their ethnicity upon arriving in a new land, and anti-Semitism is certainly one of the peculiarities that has been associated with our Southern culture. Lack of documentation notwithstanding, threads of unverifiable evidence and a gut feeling were making me wonder if I had stumbled across the unrecorded vestiges of an American pogrom.

I will most assuredly keep digging through history books and records and contacting sources that might have some insight into this and hope to one day be able to substantiate my theory, if there is indeed something to it. In the meantime, the dead will have to speak for themselves, and it may be from the ghosts of those slain for remaining "Loyal to the Union" that we are ultimately able to learn the full truth behind the Nueces Massacre.

Names on the *Treüe der Union* Monument

Following are the names that appear on the monument and grave marker in Comfort, including date and place of death and, in some cases, notes.

Ludwig Bauer, 10 August 1862, Nueces River
F. Behrens, 10 August 1862, Nueces River
Ernst Beseler, 10 August 1862, Nueces River
Conrad Bock, Captured and Murdered, Fredericksburg
Louis Boerner, 10 August 1862, Nueces River, Comfort
Wilhelm Boerner, Captured and Murdered, Comfort
Peter Bonnet, 18 October 1862, Rio Grande, Comfort
Theo Bruckisch, Captured and Murdered
Albert Bruns, 10 August 1862, Nueces River
Hilmar Degener, 10 August 1862, Nueces River
Hugo Degener, 10 August 1862, Nueces River
Pablo Diaz, 10 August 1862, Nueces River
Joseph Elstner, 18 October 1862, Rio Grande
Edward Felsing, 18 October 1862, Rio Grande
Herman Flick, Captured and Murdered, Fredericksburg
H. Herrmann, 18 October 1862, Rio Grande
V. Hohmann, 18 October 1862, Rio Grande
J. H. Kallenberg, 10 August 1862, Nueces River, Fredericksburg
Fritz Lange, 18 October 1862, Rio Grande, Comfort
August Luckenbach, Captured and Murdered, Fredericksburg
Henry Markwardt, 10 August 1862, Nueces River,
    Sisterdale, Cherry Spring
A. Ruebsamen, Captured and Murdered
L. Ruebsamen, Captured and Murdered

Christian Schaefer Sr., 10 August 1862, Nueces River, Fredericksburg
Louis Schierholz, 10 August 1862, Nueces River
Emil Schreiner, 10 August 1862, Nueces River, Kerrville
Heinrich Steves, 10 August 1862, Nueces River, Comfort
Heinrich Stieler, Captured and Murdered, Comfort
F. Tays, Captured and Murdered, Comfort
Wilhelm Telgmann, 10 August 1862, Nueces River
A. Vater, 10 August 1862, Nueces River
F. Vater, 10 August 1862, Nueces River
H. Weyershausen, 10 August 1862, Nueces River
M. Weyrich, 10 August 1862, Nueces River
Frank Weiss, 18 October 1862, Rio Grande
Moritz Weiss, 18 October 1862, Rio Grande

CHAPTER 27

Jacob's Well
HAYS COUNTY

PEERING INTO THE MYSTERIOUS and ominously beautiful depths of Jacob's Well, it is almost hard to believe that it is not haunted. Native Indians certainly held this natural artesian spring, which rises up through a limestone tube from the unmeasured depths of the underworld, to be sacred and inhabited by elemental spirits of the land. Beyond its appearance and hallowed nature, however, it is also the site of numerous drownings, and there are those who believe the ghosts of those who have perished at this spot continue to haunt it.

Jacob's Well, the mouth of the spring that forms the headwaters of aptly named Cypress Creek northwest of the village of Wimberley, has traditionally served as a swimming hole for locals living on the adjacent properties. Today it is a natural area that is open to the public and still a popular swimming spot—albeit one that is closed for several months a year so that it can recover from the environmental damage inflicted by people who use it.

While the spring coming up through Jacob's Well remains a significant source of water for people living in the area, its flow is by no means as profound as it once was. In 1924, for example, so much water surged up through the spring that it shot 6 feet into the air and its discharge was measured at 170 gallons per second. Today, however, as the result of development in the region and the heavy burden placed on the local aquifers, the flow of water from its depths manifests itself only as a faint ripple on the surface of the pool. It has even stopped flowing twice in the past couple of decades, the first times it has done so in recorded history, first in 2000 and then again in 2008. In an attempt to help protect the viability of the spring, Hays County purchased 50 acres of land around Jacob's Well, and the Wimberley Valley Watershed Association subsequently transferred an additional 31 acres from the natural area to the county.

At its mouth, Jacob's Well is 12 feet in diameter and descends vertically for about 30 feet, at which point it disappears into the darkness of the limestone caverns from which it issues. Thereafter it descends at an angle through a series of four silted chambers separated by narrow passageways to a depth of about 120 feet. The first two chambers are relatively safe and manageable for trained divers, but the next two are increasingly dangerous, with hazards that include loose debris in both and a dead end in one that can be confused with the exit tunnel and led one diver to become trapped and killed in 1983. After the fourth chamber, the cavern becomes a tunnel that continues for about 4,300 feet (e.g., more than 0.8 mile). At least one large secondary trunk splits off from this main passageway and extends for about another 1,000 feet.

Many divers have been drawn to explore and map these water-filled subterranean tunnels, but, because many of them do not have the necessary experience or equipment and the area is inherently hazardous, at least nine of them have died here since the 1970s.

"This is the horror story side of it," Don Dibble, a dive shop owner with more than four decades of diving experience, said in a 2001 interview with writer Louie Bond. "Jacob's Well definitely has a national reputation of being one of the most dangerous places to dive."

"Dibble has pulled most of the victims' remains out of Jacob's Well himself, and he nearly lost his own life in a 1979 recovery dive," Bond wrote. "Dibble was attempting to retrieve the remains of two young divers . . . when he became trapped, buried past his waist in the sliding gravel lining the bottom of the well's third chamber. Just as he ran out of air, Dibble was rescued by other divers but suffered a ruptured stomach during his rapid, unconscious ascent."

Dibble tried to block access to the entrance of the third chamber by constructing a grate made from rebar and quickset concrete in early 1980. Six months later, however, he discovered not just that the barrier had been removed but that the well-equipped people who did so had taken the time to taunt him.

"You can't keep us out," they wrote on a plastic board that they left behind for him. Perhaps not. But, in the case of some of them, inexperience, bad luck, the guardian spirits of the spring, or some combination of those things have ensured that they did not leave.

"We were not looking for human remains," Dan Misiaszek of the San Marcos Area Recovery Team wrote in his account of a 2000 foray into the perilous fourth chamber. "I first noticed one femur bone, then a second, and as I descended into the keyhole-shaped tunnel, I could see a heavily corroded scuba tank and wetsuit. It was obvious we had stumbled upon some human remains . . . The tank was still attached to a [wet suit] with weight belt." Nearby he found a human skull and, further on, evidence pointing to the identity of the person who had suffered a terrifying death there, alone and in the impenetrable darkness that would have been imposed by the disturbed silt.

Ironically, it is the reduced force of the spring that has in recent times allowed people to dive into it, and prior to the 1970s, the flow of water would have largely prevented them from doing so; people using makeshift gear attempted to descend into the spring in the 1930s, for example, but the deepest they were able to go was about 25 feet. None of them is reported to have been killed. It is almost as if a reduction of the striking site's inherent power has led to a proportionate increase in its lethality.

"It's a very mysterious place, a place of constant sensation," said author Stephen Harrigan, who wrote an acclaimed 1984 novel titled *Jacob's Well* that explores the death of a diver at the site.

I can only agree with Harrigan. Staring into Jacob's Well when I visited the site in early September 2014 was like looking into an eye that was the window to the soul of Texas Hill Country itself. After a point, it was hard not to blink or look away, and I half expected to see the shades of the dead or elemental spirits of the land swimming up toward me from the primordial depths. That they reside there is something I do not doubt.

Ghosthunting Travel Guide

AMERICA'S

HAUNTED ROAD TRIP

Visiting Haunted Sites

EACH OF THE HAUNTED SITES in this book is located in one of four general areas—the city of San Antonio, one of the seven counties comprising the Greater San Antonio area, the state capital of Austin, or Texas Hill Country. While we have gone to great efforts to verify all the information that appears here, ghosthunters are advised to confirm anything they need to know before heading into the field. Websites have been provided when available; prefixes like *http://* and *www.* are extraneous for most of the URLs that appear here and have been removed for ease of typing by readers, but have been included when necessary to make pages load properly.

Updates to this section also can be found at the Ghosthunting San Antonio, Austin, and Texas Hill Country blog (**ghost hunting-san-antonio.blogspot.com**).

CITY OF SAN ANTONIO

LOCATED IN SOUTH-CENTRAL TEXAS, San Antonio serves as the seat of Bexar County, has a population of 1.3 million, and is the seventh most populous city in the United States and the second most populous city in the state of Texas. A 1691 Spanish expedition to the area celebrated mass here on June 13, feast day of Saint Anthony of Padua, and named the new settlement for him. San Antonio is notable for Spanish colonial missions, the Alamo, the River Walk, the annual San Antonio Stock Show and Rodeo, and the Tower of the Americas and is visited by about 26 million tourists per year. The U.S. military has a long and substantial presence that led to San Antonio being dubbed "Military City U.S.A." and facilities that include Fort Sam Houston, Lackland Air Force

Base, Randolph Air Force Base, and Lackland AFB/Kelly Field Annex, with Camp Bullis and Camp Stanley located outside the city. With a colorful and violent history of colonialism, Indian raids, wars of independence, filibuster invasions, and more, it is little wonder that San Antonio is home to so many reputedly haunted places.

SAN ANTONIO MISSIONS NATIONAL HISTORICAL PARK
South and Downtown San Antonio
2202 Roosevelt Ave.
San Antonio, TX 78210
210-932-1001; **nps.gov/saan**
HOURS: Daily, 9 a.m.–5 p.m., unless otherwise noted

OF THE ORIGINAL six Spanish missions founded along the banks of the San Antonio River, four are them—Mission Concepción, Mission San Jose, Mission San Juan, and Mission Espada, in geographic order from north (upstream of the San Antonio River) to south—are now part of San Antonio Missions National Historical Park. (The fifth existing site, the Alamo, is administered separately, while the remains of a sixth, Mission Najera, are now located on a local golf course). Espada Aqueduct, also part of the park, is due east of and across the river from Mission San Juan.

Mission Concepción
807 Mission Road
San Antonio, TX 78210

Mission San José
6701 San Jose Drive
San Antonio, TX 78214
FOUNDED IN 1720, this location was designated as the San José Mission National Historic Site in 1941.

Mission San Juan
9101 Graf Road
San Antonio, TX 78214
MISSION SAN JUAN was listed on the National Register of Historic Places on February 23, 1972, and has been maintained by the National Park Service since the 1980s.

Mission Espada
10040 Espada Road
San Antonio, TX 78214
THIS MISSION WAS LISTED on the National Register of Historic Places on February 23, 1972.

THE ALAMO Downtown San Antonio
300 Alamo Plaza
San Antonio, TX 78205
210-225-1391; **thealamo.org**
HOURS: Daily, 9 a.m.–5:30 p.m. (7 p.m. in the summer).
THIS BEST-KNOWN MISSION in San Antonio is located downtown, owned by the state of Texas, and operated by the Daughters of the Republic of Texas. Witnesses claim to see the spirits of various defenders of the mission since almost immediately after the 1836 battle for which it is famous.

ALAMODOME Downtown San Antonio
100 Montana St.
San Antonio, TX 78203
210-207-3663; **alamodome.com**
HOURS: Variable depending on the event
THE ALAMODOME OPENED on May 15, 1993, and was the home of the NBA World Champion San Antonio Spurs until 2002. In addition to hosting basketball and football, with seating for 65,000, it is also used as a convention center and performance venue.

ALAMO QUARRY MARKET North Central San Antonio
255 E. Basse Road, Ste. 400
San Antonio, TX 78209
210-824-8885; **quarrymarket.com**
HOURS: Monday–Saturday, 10 a.m.–9 p.m.; Sunday, noon–6 p.m.
THIS SHOPPING CENTER located on the grounds of an old industrial complex includes numerous stores, restaurants, and a cinema.

COMANCHE LOOKOUT PARK Northeast San Antonio
15551 Nacogdoches Road
San Antonio, TX 78247
201-207-7275
sanantonio.gov/parksandrec/directory_comanche_lookout.aspx
HOURS: Daily, 5 a.m.–11 p.m.

Crockett Hotel   Downtown San Antonio
320 Bonham St.
San Antonio, TX 78205
210-225-6500; **crocketthotel.com**

BUILT IN 1909, this hotel is located on the site where Alamo defender David Crockett is believed to have been killed, and it is believed to be haunted by the ghosts of long-dead soldiers. Active areas include the lobby, the bar, and a few of the guest rooms. The front door to the lobby sometimes opens and closes on its own; many guests and staff members have seen an apparition of a man in a dark-blue jacket similar to the one worn by soldiers at the Alamo; and whispers, the sudden appearance of cold spots, and disembodied footsteps also have been reported throughout the hotel. It has 138 guest rooms and suites, a breakfast area, and a bar.

Emily Morgan Hotel   Downtown San Antonio
705 E. Houston St.
San Antonio, TX 78205
210-225-5100; **emilymorganhotel.com**

KNOWN AS "The Official Hotel of the Alamo," the Emily Morgan was built in the 1920s as the Medical Arts Building, is just blocks from San Antonio's famous River Walk, and offers stunning views of the Alamo.

Menger Hotel   Downtown San Antonio
204 Alamo Plaza
San Antonio, TX 78205
210-223-4361; **mengerhotel.com**

THIS LUXURY HOTEL, adjacent to the Alamo, first opened its doors in 1836 and is the location where Teddy Roosevelt recruited his famous Rough Riders during the Spanish-American War. It is the oldest continuously operating hotel west of the Mississippi River.

Old Bexar County Jail/Holiday Inn Express San Antonio N–Riverwalk Area   Downtown San Antonio
120 Camaron St.
San Antonio, TX 78205
210-281-1400; **holidayexpressriverwalk.com**

SAN FERNANDO CATHEDRAL   Downtown San Antonio
115 S. Main Plaza
San Antonio, TX 78205
210-227-1297; **tinyurl.com/sanfernandocathedral**
HOURS: Monday–Friday, 8 a.m.–5 p.m.; Saturday, 8 a.m.–6:30 p.m.,
   Sunday, 8 a.m.–6 p.m.
   SAN FERNANDO CATHEDRAL was founded in 1731 and is the oldest con-
   tinuously operating religious community in the state of Texas.

SHERATON GUNTER HOTEL SAN ANTONIO   Downtown San Antonio
205 E. Houston St.
San Antonio, TX 78205
210-554-1788; **sheratongunter.com**
   FORMERLY KNOWN AS the Camberly Gunter Hotel, what is now known as
   the Sheraton Gunter Hotel was built in 1909 and is in close proximity to
   the River Walk, Alamo, and other downtown attractions. Today, the historic
   hotel offers 322 guest rooms and continues to be a popular destination for
   visitors to San Antonio. It is rumored to be haunted by the ghosts of a prostitute who was murdered there and that of the man who killed her in 1965.

SPANISH GOVERNOR'S PALACE   Downtown San Antonio
105 Military Plaza
San Antonio, TX 78205
210-224-0601; **tinyurl.com/sagovernorspalace**
HOURS: Tuesday–Saturday, 9 a.m.–5 p.m.; Sunday 10 a.m.–5 p.m.

UNIVERSITY OF THE INCARNATE WORD
Alamo Heights/Midtown San Antonio
4301 Broadway St.
San Antonio, TX 78209; **uiw.edu**

VICTORIA'S BLACK SWAN INN   Northeast San Antonio
1006 Holbrook Road
San Antonio, TX 78218
210-323-8424; **victoriasblackswaninn.com**
   VICTORIA'S BLACK SWAN INN is famous as a site of multiple hauntings;
   has been featured in numerous books, articles, and television programs; is
   a popular venue for ghosthunting groups; and offers a wide array of events
   and ghost tours. Built in 1867 on the site of the September 14, 1842, Battle

of Salado, Victoria's Black Swan Inn has been a home to some of the most prestigious people in San Antonio's history, such as Park and Jolene Street. It also has hosted writers such as Erle Stanley Gardner, creator of the famed *Perry Mason* television series, and some of Texas's most famous musicians and artists.

GREATER SAN ANTONIO

THIS AREA INCLUDES THE SEVEN COUNTIES— Atascosa, Bandera, Comal, Guadalupe, Kendall, Medina, and Wilson—that surround Bexar County and the city of San Antonio, and has a population of nearly one million people. It also includes independent cities in Bexar County that are in some cases, like that of Leon Valley, completely surrounded by San Antonio. This area contains a mix of historic towns like Seguin and New Braunfels, suburbs, a handful of public parks, and lots of private ranchland.

FAUST HOTEL   New Braunfels/Comal County
240 S. Seguin Ave.
New Braunfels, TX 78130
830-625-7791; **fausthotel.com**

"LOCATED IN HISTORIC DOWNTOWN New Braunfels, the Faust Hotel was built in 1929 and offers guests a step back in time to a period of simplicity and elegance," the hotel history states. It "has been lovingly restored to its 1920s splendor with the best of modern hotel conveniences, all while preserving the original antiquity and authenticity of the architecture, decor, and ambience of the original hotel."

GRUENE HISTORIC DISTRICT   New Braunfels/Comal County
I-35 Exit 191 toward Canyon Lake
830-629-5077; **gruenetexas.com**

GRUENE IS A LIVELY LITTLE HISTORIC TOWN that boasts numerous events and activities. There are a number of outstanding restaurants, shops, and, of course, Gruene Hall, built in 1878 and the oldest continuously operating and most famous dance hall in Texas. Gruene itself has been added to the National Register of Historic Places, and many of its buildings have been awarded medallions from the Texas Historical Commission. It also has been recognized by the Texas travel industry as a premier attraction for visitors.

LA MANSION   Boerne/Kendall County

707 S. Main St.
Boerne, TX 78006
830-331-2552
HOURS: Monday–Wednesday, 8 a.m.–8 p.m.; Thursday–Saturday,
8 a.m.–9 p.m.; Sunday, 8 a.m.–8 p.m.

AROUND 1870, a French architect named Frank LaMotte constructed the
impressive limestone building on Main Street in the town of Boerne that has
since been known in the local area simply as the Mansion. Just as its name
has been carried down through the years, so too have the stories of spiritual
activity in the house and a persistent reputation for being haunted.

YE KENDALL INN   Boerne/Kendall County

128 W. Blanco Road
Boerne, TX 78006
830-249-9954; **yekendallinn.com**

ESTABLISHED AS A PRIVATE HOME in 1859 on the Boerne town square and
along the banks of Cibolo Creek, this historic stone building became a hotel in 1878 and today is a 36-room inn that is co-located with the Limestone
Grille restaurant. It is also apparently haunted, and people have reportedly
experienced strange phenomena there for years. These include hearing heavy
disembodied footsteps coming from parts of the building where no one is
present; the sound of doors opening and then slamming shut even when they
are securely locked; crystal prisms falling off of chandeliers; doorknobs rattling; and the building's electricity not working. One guest room in particular
has reportedly been the site of a number of odd events and accidents.

AUSTIN

LOCATED IN CENTRAL TEXAS, Austin is the state capi-
tal and the seat of Travis County. It has an estimated 865,504 residents and is by population the 11th-largest city in the United States,
the fourth-largest city in Texas, and the second-largest U.S. state
capital. In the 1830s, pioneers began to settle the area in central
Austin along the Colorado River and, in 1839, replaced Houston
as the capital. Initially called Waterloo, it was soon after renamed
in honor of Stephen F. Austin, the "Father of Texas." Austin grew

throughout the 19th century and became a center for government and education with the construction of the Texas State Capitol and the University of Texas at Austin. After a lull in growth during the Great Depression, Austin resumed its development and, by the 1980s, emerged as a center for technology and business. Austinites include a diverse mix of government employees, college students, musicians, high-tech and blue-collar workers, and businesspeople. Its nicknames have included "Silicon Hills," "Live Music Capital of the World," and "City of the Violet Crown" for the wintertime violet glow of color across the hills just after sunset. Its unofficial slogan is "Keep Austin Weird." Considering its long, strange, and colorful history, it should not be surprising that Austin is home to innumerable haunted sites.

Austin Pizza Garden   Oak Hill/Southwest Austin
6266 W. Highway 290
Austin, TX 78735
512-891-9980; **austin-pizza-garden.com**
Hours: Sunday–Thursday, 11 a.m.–10 p.m.; Friday–Saturday, 11 a.m.–11 p.m.
> **This gourmet pizza restaurant** is located in a historic 19th-century limestone structure that was originally used as a general store and is believed to be haunted by the spirits of a number of its former residents.

Driskill Hotel   Downtown Austin
604 Brazos St.
Austin, TX 78701
512-391-7039; **driskillhotel.com**
> **Built in 1886** and located in the heart of downtown Austin, this luxurious, historic hotel is convenient to the Texas State Capitol, convention center, opera, symphony, fine dining, shopping, and Austin's Sixth Street music scene. It also is reputed to be an ongoing haunt for a number of troubled spirits.

Richard Moya Park/Moore's Crossing Bridge
   Southwest Austin
10001 Burleson Road
Austin, TX 78719
512-854-7275; **parks.traviscountytx.gov/find-a-park/richard-moya**

This 11.55-acre park is located along the banks of Onion Creek, about 10 miles southeast of downtown Austin, off of one of the roads that runs past the south side of Austin-Bergstrom International Airport. Located within it is a bridge that once crossed the Colorado River near the capitol and upon which the shades of the dead are sometimes reported.

TEXAS STATE CAPITOL   Downtown Austin
1100 Congress Ave.
Austin, TX 78701
512-463-8400; **www.tspb.state.tx.us**
HOURS: Monday–Friday, 7 a.m.–10 p.m.; Saturday and Sunday 9 a.m.–8 p.m. Hours are extended during legislative sessions. Closed Thanksgiving Day, Christmas Eve Day, Christmas Day, New Year's Day, and Easter.

DESIGNED IN 1881 and completed in 1888, the Texas Capitol is located in downtown Austin and contains the office of the governor and the offices and chambers of the state legislature. It should hardly be surprising that the capitol of a state that has historically been so marked by violence, corruption, and zealous ideologies as Texas should have a wealth of ghostly lore and strange phenomena associated with it. Tours are available free of charge, and a special "Rest in Peace" tour is offered up to twice a day during the month of October.

TEXAS STATE CAPITOL VISITORS CENTER   Downtown Austin
112 E. 11th St.
Austin, TX 78701
512-305-6400; **www.tspb.state.tx.us/CVC/home/home.html**
HOURS: Monday–Saturday 9 a.m.–5 p.m., Sunday noon–5 p.m. Closed Thanksgiving Day, Christmas Eve Day, Christmas Day, New Year's Day, and Easter.

THIS STRUCTURE, which originally served as the General Land Office Building, was added to the National Register of Historic Places in 1970 and recognized as a National Historic Landmark in 1986.

UNIVERSITY OF TEXAS TOWER   Downtown Austin
Texas Union Hospitality Center
24th and Guadalupe Streets (2247 Guadalupe St.)
Austin, TX 78713-7338
512-475-6633; **utexas.edu/tower**
ON AUGUST 1, 1966, a 25-year-old former marine who was an architectural engineering student at the University of Texas ascended its tower and

launched a bloody rampage from its observation deck that left 18 people dead and 42 wounded. Some people have sensed the presence of a deranged spirit in and around the tower and believe it to be that of the killer. There is also a garden on the site "dedicated to the memory of all those who died and those whose lives were touched by the . . . shooting." Nine years after the attack, in 1975, this event was commemorated in an NBC made-for-TV movie called *The Deadly Tower*, in which Kurt Russell plays the deranged gunman.

TEXAS HILL COUNTRY

EXACTLY WHAT TEXAS HILL COUNTRY comprises can vary a lot depending on whom you ask! According to the Texas Heritage Trails Program, it is "a geographically diverse 19-county area that abounds with natural resources. From tranquil lakes and rivers fed by underground springs, to canyons, hills and roadways hewn from the natural limestone; from lush fields brimming with the fruits of her rich earth, to the plentiful wildlife that roams free." The Texas Parks and Wildlife Department, however, expands this area by a half-dozen counties, and its definition of Hill Country includes a full 25 of them. For our purposes, this area includes Bell, Blanco, Burnet, Coryell, Crockett, Edwards, Gillespie, Hays, Kerr, Kimble, Lampasas, Llano, Mason, McCullouch, Menard, Real, San Saba, Schleicher, Sutton, Travis, Val Verde, and Williamson Counties. This area is full of historic towns and villages; state, local, and national wilderness areas; lots of ranchland surrounded by fences hung with unwelcoming signage; and plenty of haunted places. A handful of examples follow, but just ask the staff at any two establishments in historical towns and villages in this area, and chances are at least one of them will have a ghost story associated with it.

DEVIL'S BACKBONE **Blanco County, Comal County, Hays County**
Ranch-to-Market Road 32 (From where it intersects with RM 12, just south of Wimberley, west about 24 miles to where it intersects with Highway 281, just south of Blanco).

THIS HAUNTED HIGHWAY corresponds with a ridgeline used by Spanish explorers traveling inland and later by ranchers driving cattle. At several points, such as near the little Blanco River, there are good places to pull over, park, and walk around. Watch out, however, for anyone who might be driving too fast down RM 32 if you do get out of your car or slow down to enjoy the scenery! There are few amenities available along RM 32, so be sure to take any snacks or drinks you might want to have with you. And, as it is a relatively isolated area, be sure to have a cell phone with you as well if you own one (reception does not appear to be a problem along most of the road).

Devil's Backbone Tavern
4041 FM 32
Fischer, TX 78623
830-964-2544
HOURS: Noon–midnight (or later)
ANOTHER SPOT ALONG the haunted highway that travelers might want to visit is the Devil's Backbone Tavern, a watering hole located on the site of an old Indian campground and what was once a stagecoach stop. It is patronized by ranchers, bikers, and locals who have included late author Bert Wall, and it even became the subject of the "Ballad of the Devil's Backbone Tavern" after musician Todd Snider spent a summer in the 1980s performing there on Friday nights.

ENCHANTED ROCK   Gillespie County, Llano County
16710 Ranch Road 965
Fredericksburg, TX 78624
830-685-3636; **tpwd.state.tx.us/state-parks/enchanted-rock**
HOURS: Daily, 8 a.m.–10 p.m.
ENCHANTED ROCK STATE NATURAL AREA is part of the Texas state park system and includes 1,644 acres designated as a Recorded Texas Historic Landmark in 1936. This area is 18 miles north of Fredericksburg and sits on Big Sandy Creek at the border of Gillespie and Llano counties. More than 250,000 people trek to the park each year to experience the magic of Enchanted Rock, and it is one of the most visited sites in the state park system. Scheduled Summit Trail tours are available during the third Saturday of the month in April, May, September, October, November, and December, and private tours are available for groups at other times. Emphasis is placed on activity safety and ecological preservation, and visitors are asked to keep

human incursion at a minimum by not disturbing plants, animals, or artifacts. There is a $7 entrance fee.

Jacob's Well Natural Area
Hays County
1699 Mount Sharp Road
Wimberley, TX 78676
512-847-2140; **www.co.hays.tx.us/jwna.aspx**
HOURS: Sunday–Saturday, 10 a.m.–8 p.m.
JACOB'S WELL is an artesian spring located just north of the village of Wimberley. Water flows up through it from the Trinity Aquifer some 140 feet below the surface. It features layered limestone cliffs on one side, a vibrantly
vegetated bank on the other, a lively riparian area alongside the creek, and,
according to some, the spirits of those who have died horribly in its depths.

JAMES KIEHL RIVER BEND PARK/SA&AP BRIDGE
COMFORT/KENDALL COUNTY
118 River Bend Road
Comfort, TX 78013; **kendallcountyparks.org/parks/james-kiehl-river-bend-park**
HOURS: Daily, 7 a.m.–dusk
JAMES KIEHL RIVER BEND PARK is a pleasant, 25-acre recreational area
situated along the banks of the Guadalupe River. Paranormal phenomena
have been noted both at it and at a disused railway bridge located nearby.

Treüe der Union Monument
Comfort/Kendall County
High Street (between Third and Fourth Streets)
Comfort, TX 78013
830-995-2641.
ONE OF THE STRANGEST, bloodiest, and most heartbreaking episodes in
the saga of a violent state took place during the Civil War and is commemorated with the *Treüe der Union* or "Loyalty to the Union" monument in the historic village of Comfort. There is every reason to think it might be haunted by
the spirits of those whose deaths it memorializes and whose remains it marks.

Additional Haunted Sites

THIS SECTION CONTAINS nearly five dozen reputedly haunted sites throughout San Antonio, Austin, and Texas Hill Country beyond those given a detailed treatment elsewhere in this book and which, for various reasons, are not included among them but are still significant enough to warrant at least brief coverage.

In some cases, the reason an entry might appear here is simply that there was not room to devote entire chapters to as many sites as we would have liked. In other cases, sites in the following section might not be as easy to visit or investigate as is necessary for them to be given feature treatment. There can be various reasons for this, ranging from them being public sites with management that does not encourage paranormal investigation, to sites that are closed but can still be investigated from outside, to sites with selectively restricted access (for example, military installations). They may thus not be as user-friendly as those to which full chapters are devoted, and readers should bear this in mind when planning visits to them.

Websites have been provided when available; prefixes like *http://* and *www.* are extraneous for most of the URLs that appear here and have been removed for ease of typing by readers, but have been included when necessary to make pages load properly.

Some of these sites also receive more detailed treatment at the official Ghosthunting San Antonio, Austin, and Texas Hill Country blog (**ghosthunting-san-antonio.blogspot.com**).

CITY OF SAN ANTONIO

ALAMO METHODIST CHURCH   Downtown San Antonio
1150 S. Alamo St.
San Antonio, TX 78210

THIS BUILDING IN THE King William Historic District was built in 1912 and served as home to the Alamo Methodist Church until 1968, after which it was vacant until 1976, when it was reopened as the Alamo Street Theater and Restaurant. As of this writing, the latter establishment had shut down and the building was for sale. At least four ghosts are believed to haunt the building, including those of Margaret Gething, an actress who lived in the neighborhood; Eddie, a young boy who enjoys moving things, playing pranks, turning lights on and off, and making noise; a man in early-20th-century clothing who may have been a member of the congregation that worshipped here; and Henrietta, a seamstress and Margaret Gething's servant, who is believed to move costumes around. Other highlights of the site include the original Tiffany stained glass windows and tin ceiling.

BROOKS CITY BASE   Southeast San Antonio
3201 Sidney Brooks Drive
San Antonio, TX 78235
210-678-3300; **www.brookscity-base.com**

ESTABLISHED AS A TRAINING CAMP toward the end of World War I in 1918 in what is now downtown San Antonio, this installation, formerly known as Brooks Air Force Base, was closed down in September 2011. It was named in honor of Sidney Johnson Brooks Jr., an American Flying Corps cadet who was killed in a training accident on November 13, 1917. Areas of what is now a cutting-edge industrial park that are currently accessible to the public include Hangar 9, a World War I–era structure that now houses the U.S. Air Force Museum of Aerospace Medicine. According to some reports, on foggy nights a spectral young woman with a backpack can be seen walking around the site, sometimes waking sleeping security personnel by tapping them on the shoulder!

CADILLAC BAR RESTAURANT   Downtown San Antonio
212 S. Flores St.
San Antonio, TX 78204
210-223-5533; **sawhost.com/cadillac**

ORIGINS OF THE Cadillac Bar Restaurant can be traced back to New Orleans in the early 1920s. Prohibition induced the original owner to relocate the establishment to Nuevo Laredo, Mexico, in 1926, and to return to the United States and set up shop in San Antonio once liquor could be legally sold there again. It is now located in Stumberg Square in a building that dates to the 1870s and was originally a general store that was a favorite meeting place for local farmers and ranchers. Behind the store was a camp yard for wagons and livestock. In 1914, what are believed to be the first electric streetlights in Texas were installed to illuminate this area, and these are still used today in what is now a brick courtyard behind the restaurant.

At least two ghosts have been reported to haunt the establishment by restaurant staff. One is the spirit of a previous owner, whom people claim to have seen in a basement storage area. The other is reputedly the "negative spirit" of a former employee named Beatrice who was unhappy in life and who now does things like throw kitchen utensils and turn on water taps.

CHINESE GRAVEYARD   Southside San Antonio
10359–10445 S. Zarzamora St.
San Antonio, TX 78224

THIS SMALL, DESOLATE BURIAL GROUND is easy to miss, so drive slowly if looking for it. Local legends claim that if anyone parks inside the site and then flashes their headlights quickly five times that they will hear disembodied voices and see white apparitions appear; perhaps related to this are strange pale mists that people have reported seeing here. Visitors have also reported signs of occult activity and of being chased off by one or more black-clad people.

ST. ANTHONY HOTEL   Downtown San Antonio
300 E. Travis St.
San Antonio, TX 78205
210-227-4392; **thestanthonyhotel.com**

THREE AMBITIOUS CATTLEMEN, A. H. Jones, B. L. Naylor, and F. M. Swearingen, opened the St. Anthony Hotel in 1909 in anticipation of San Antonio becoming a tourist destination, and it quickly became a popular place for visitors to stay. It is located near San Antonio's River Walk and the Alamo. "Not only was it the first luxury hotel in the city, but in the early days it was also the only inn with air conditioning, a drive-up registration desk, and sophisticated automatic doors and lights," the official history of the hotel states. "In fact, St. Anthony was so technologically savvy that it was con-

sidered among the world's most modern hotels. By 1915, the hotel charged guests $1.50 per night, and booming revenues allowed the owners to double capacity to 430 guestrooms."

Many rich and famous Americans were among the visitors to the St. Anthony, its restaurant, and its bar. They have included Fred Astaire, Lucille Ball, George Clooney, President Dwight D. Eisenhower, Judy Garland, Greer Garson, Rock Hudson, Betty Hutton, General Douglas McArthur, Matthew McConaughey, Demi Moore, Gregory Peck, Prince Rainier and Princess Grace of Monaco, Mickey Rooney, Eleanor Roosevelt, John Wayne, Arnold Schwarzenegger, Maria Shriver, Patrick Swayze, and Bruce Willis.

Paranormal phenomena people have experienced at the St. Anthony Hotel include seeing strange shadowy outlines, feeling unseen presences, seeing doors opening and closing for no apparent reason, and hearing disembodied footsteps following behind them.

DEVIL's BRIDGE   Southeast San Antonio
2450 E. Ashley Road
San Antonio, TX 78214

WHAT IS COLLOQUIALLY known by many in the local area as the Devil's Bridge is technically called the Bergs Mill Veterans Memorial Bridge and is "Dedicated to the Men and Women Who Served in the Military." This former automobile span has been converted for foot traffic and is located along a fairly desolate stretch of road at the south end of San Antonio and just a little ways from the Mission San Juan National Park (which is the most convenient

place to park for those interested in visiting the bridge). Some visitors have claimed that it is unnaturally dark beneath the bridge and that when they have thrown rocks under it they cannot hear them land.

FORT SAM HOUSTON
NORTHEAST SAN ANTONIO
San Antonio, TX 78234
210-221-1211; **samhouston.army.mil**

BUILT IN 1876 at the height of the Indian Wars and named for the first president of the Republic of Texas, Fort Sam Houston is a historic U.S. Army installation and one of the service's oldest. It was designated a National Historic Landmark in 1975 and contains numerous haunted structures and accounts of paranormal activity. The oldest part of the installation is the Quadrangle, now an office complex housing the commanding general and staff of U.S. Army North command but originally constructed as a supply depot and used at one point to house Apache war chief Geronimo and the warriors captured with him. Legend has it that the game animals were kept in the Quadrangle because Geronimo refused to eat food he did not hunt, but for reasons that are now unclear, deer and peacocks were kept there even prior to his confinement. Other sections of the installation represent different eras of construction and reflect various Army concepts in planning and design. They have been carefully preserved.

Paranormal phenomena reported in various historic structures on the post include sensing disembodied footsteps, detecting the presence of a ghostly child who moves objects around, and inexplicably hearing the sound of a piano playing.

GHOST TRACKS   Southside San Antonio
Shane and Villamain Roads
San Antonio, TX 78214

ONE OF THE MOST OMNIPRESENT urban legends in San Antonio is that of the Ghost Tracks, which combines elements of tragic death, haunting, and the "gravity hills" that can be found in many other places. The site associated with the story is located at the intersection of Shane and Villamain Roads, not far from Espada Park in Southside San Antonio and just 0.3 mile beyond the southern edge of Interstate 410.

According to most versions of the tale, in the 1920s or 1930s, a school bus carrying students home was crossing the tracks at this point when it became stuck and was then struck by a train and all the children riding on it killed. Some people believe that the spirits of the children now haunt the site and that there are a number of ways to detect their presence. The most common means of doing so is for a visitor to put a car in neutral up to 100 yards away from the tracks, upon which it will appear to roll uphill and across the tracks, ostensibly being pushed by the spirits of the children. Those who attempt this experiment also sometimes put flour or baby powder on the bumpers, hoods, or backs of their cars, and some claim that tiny handprints can then be found in it.

There are a number of popular variants on this story. One maintains that those visiting the site at nightfall on the anniversary of the original incident will see the crossing guard arms come down and the warning lights start to blink, and then will hear and feel an unseen train rushing by and have their car pushed back several feet even if it is in park. There are, however, some significant problems with this version of the tale, one being that no one can agree on the year the wreck happened, much less the specific date—and the other being that there are no crossing guards or lights at the site!

Some visitors claim to feel an oppressive, even satanic presence in the area, but this would not seem to be compatible with the back story or most common paranormal phenomena associated with the location. Paranormal investigators are, perhaps understandably, somewhat leery of this site and the stories associated with it. John Delgado of San Antonio Ghost Hunters, for example, told me that there is nothing to the story of the ghostly children—but did note that ghostly presences can sometimes be detected in the area because local gangs have long used the surrounding woods as a place to dump the bodies of their victims!

Hot Wells Hotel and Spa   Southside San Antonio
Koehler Court
San Antonio, TX 78223

> THIS ELEGANT HOTEL AND SPA, dating to the 1890s, once attracted the rich and famous from around the country. It was destroyed in a series of three fires, in 1925, 1988, and 1997, and is now a sprawling and haunted ruin. Visitors have reported various paranormal phenomena at the site, including smelling the stench of burnt flesh.

Hotel Indigo San Antonio Downtown-Alamo
  Downtown San Antonio
105 N. Alamo St.
San Antonio, TX 78205
210-933-2000; **ihg.com** (search for San Antonio locations and select "Hotel Indigo Downtown Alamo"; do not confuse with Hotel Indigo San Antonio–Riverwalk)

> THIS HISTORIC HOTEL is located at what had once been the northwest corner of the Alamo compound, site of the bloodiest fighting when Mexican troops overran the mission and slaughtered its Texian defenders on March 6, 1836. Garrison commander William B. Travis was among those who fell here (the front desk being located at the spot where he was believed to have died), and it was so packed with mangled bodies in the aftermath of the battle that the ground was said to have been saturated with blood.
>
>
>
> In the years after the battle, Samuel Maverick, who left the besieged Alamo four days before it fell to serve as a delegate to the convention for Texas independence, built his home at this location. Then, in 1909, Southern Pacific Railroad executive Colonel C. C. Gibbs built the first skyscraper in San Antonio on the site. The Gibbs building

still stands today and houses the beautiful Hotel Indigo San Antonio Downtown-Alamo.

Paranormal activity people claim to experience at the hotel includes hearing the sounds of gun and cannon fire and the agonized wailing of wounded and dying men; seeing spectral figures moving a cannon along the adjacent streets; hearing strange voices and disembodied footsteps, particularly in the basement; seeing people getting on and off the historic and now out-of-service elevators; and witnessing figures in 19th-century clothing walking down the halls, entering rooms, and then disappearing.

INSTITUTE OF TEXAN CULTURE   Downtown San Antonio
801 E. Cesar E. Chavez Blvd.
San Antonio, TX 78205-3296
210-458-2300; **texancultures.com**

ESTABLISHED IN 1968, this museum and library located in HemisFair Park serves as the state's primary center for multicultural education, with exhibits, programs, and events like the annual Texas Folklife Festival. The facility originally served as the Texas Pavilion at the 1968 World's Fair. Numerous accounts of paranormal activity have been reported here, including the unexplained smell of pipe smoke, disembodied footsteps near the audio/visual room, books being mysteriously rearranged in the library, and the back of an 1898 glass hearse opening on its own.

MARRIOTT PLAZA SAN ANTONIO   Downtown San Antonio
555 S. Alamo St.
San Antonio, TX 78205
210-229-1000; **marriott.com/hotels/travel/satpl-marriott-plaza-san-antonio**

THIS DOWNTOWN HOTEL is in close proximity to the Alamo, has a number of historic buildings on its grounds, and—like many old sites with storied pasts—has many ghosts and inexplicable phenomena associated with it. Reported activity ranges from things like lights turning on and off on their own to drawers at the front desk being opened as if by an unseen hand to a specter who has haunted the hotel for many years and come to be known as the Lady. She is believed to be a widow who lived in one of the historic buildings now incorporated into the hotel and to have hanged herself and her cat in what is now the exercise facility, formerly her parlor. People have reported seeing her throughout the site, especially on the upper levels of the main building, in the employee-only areas in the basement, or standing among the trees in the garden, usually in a long white dress or gown, holding her cat and stroking its head.

McNay Art Museum   Near East Side San Antonio

6000 N. New Braunfels Ave.
San Antonio, TX 78209
210-824-5368; **mcnayart.org**

In 1926, eight years after she first visited the city, when her late husband
was serving with the U.S. Army in Laredo, Texas, Ohio-born heiress Marion
Koogler McNay moved to San Antonio and there met and married prominent ophthalmologist Donald T. Atkinson. The following year, she and her
husband commissioned two local architects to design the 24-room Spanish
Colonial Revival house that would one day become the core of the McNay
Art Museum. She also purchased her first modern oil painting and continued to collect 19th- and 20th-century European and American paintings and
Southwest art from New Mexico. She resumed using her first husband's
name when her marriage to Atkinson ended in 1936. When she died in 1950,
McNay left her collection of more than 700 works of art, the house and
the 23 acres upon which it is located, and an endowment to establish the
first museum of modern art in Texas. In 1954, the institution opened to the
public, and in 2008, it was expanded with the addition of gallery space for
major exhibitions, a sculpture gallery and garden, a lecture hall, and class-
rooms for educational programs. Today the museum houses almost 20,000
works, including Medieval and Renaissance art; 19th- through 21st-century
European and American paintings, sculptures, and photographs; one of the
finest collections of prints and drawings in the Southwest; a collection of
theater arts; a collection of art glass; and art of New Mexico.

McNay's spirit is believed to haunt the museum that bears her name,
possibly curating in death the collection of art that meant so much to her
in life. Museum staff and security personnel in particular are among those
who claim to have seen her shade gliding down the halls, passing through
walls, and levitating from one building to another, generally during hours
of darkness. Witnesses also claim to see McNay look at them and to hear a
female voice humming a tune, particularly in the museum library.

North Star Mall   Castle Hills/Uptown San Antonio

7400 San Pedro Ave.
San Antonio, TX 78216-5358
210-340-6627; **northstarmall.com**

PARANORMAL PHENOMENA reported at North Star Mall, near the intersection of two main highways and right across from San Antonio International Air-

port, would suggest that it is built on the site of earlier structures and events. Witnesses have reported seeing "shadow people" in the facility, and employees say that they have heard their names whispered in their ears.

OAK VALLEY VINEYARDS TEXAS BISTRO   Far North Side San Antonio
27315 Natural Bridge Caverns Road
San Antonio, TX 78266
830-980-8033; **oakvalleyvineyardsrestaurant.com**

THIS FINE-DINING RESTAURANT, surrounded by fields of grapevines, has wonderful rustic elegance and, apparently, ghosts as well, and various local paranormal investigation groups have taken an interest in it.

OUR LADY OF THE LAKE UNIVERSITY   Inner West Side San Antonio
411 SW 24th St.
San Antonio, TX 78207
210-434-6711; **ollusa.edu**

OUR LADY OF THE LAKE UNIVERSITY is a small Catholic private school with a lakeside campus that was founded in 1895 by the Sisters of the Congregation of Divine Providence. It was the first San Antonio institution of higher education to receive regional accreditation, and its Worden School of Social Service is the oldest school of social work in Texas. Its campus includes many historic buildings, some of which are believed to still be occupied by the spirits of former students and staff, among them ghostly nuns and a janitor who is said to now haunt the basement of the library.

RIVER CENTER MALL   Downtown San Antonio
849 E. Commerce St.
San Antonio, TX 78205
210-225-0000; **shoprivercenter.com**

ONE DOES NOT USUALLY THINK of a mall as being a likely venue for ghosts, but then most malls are not built on the site of major battlefields as is this one, which is adjacent to the haunted Alamo, Menger Hotel, and Crockett Hotel. Paranormal activity here includes lights turning off and on by themselves and books being moved around in a bookstore that used to be located in the lower level of the mall. People have frequently reported greater activity here on March 6, the anniversary of the Battle of the Alamo. There is evidence, in fact, that this section of the mall corresponds to the location of one of the funeral pyres on which the Texian defenders of the Alamo were burned.

SAN ANTONIO RIVER WALK   Downtown San Antonio
210-227-4262; **thesanantonioriverwalk.com**

ALSO KNOWN AS PASEO DEL RÍO, the San Antonio River Walk is a network of walkways along the banks of the San Antonio River, one story beneath the streets of Downtown San Antonio. It is an enormously successful special-case pedestrian street and public park that is lined by bars, shops, and restaurants and is an important part of the city's urban fabric and a tourist attraction in its own right. The River Walk winds and loops under bridges as two parallel sidewalks, connecting major tourist draws from the Alamo to Rivercenter Mall, the Arneson River Theatre, Marriage Island, La Villita, HemisFair Park, the Tower Life Building, the San Antonio Museum of Art, and the Pearl Brewery.

Because it flows through and is surrounded by haunted sites and has been the location of many deaths over the years—one of the worst episodes being the flood of 1921, which claimed at least 50 lives—the River Walk itself can well be said to be haunted, and over the years many people have reported episodes of paranormal activity on it. Some of the stranger things seen are spirits in the San Antonio River itself, including ones of fish that people claim have spoken to them.

SAN PEDRO SPRINGS PARK   Downtown San Antonio
1415 San Pedro Ave.
San Antonio, TX 78212
210-207-7275; **sanantonio.gov/parksandrec/directory_san_pedro.aspx**

SAN PEDRO SPRINGS PARK is San Antonio's oldest designated park and is located on land reserved for public use by the Spanish government in the 18th century. People have gathered around the springs and creek that originate here

for some 12,000 years. Considering its age and continuous use by humans, it is little wonder that paranormal phenomena of all sorts have been reported at this 46-acre recreational area. One thing numerous people claim to have seen is children in 1930s-era school uniforms playing in the park who, when one turns away from them momentarily, abruptly disappear.

Wikimedia Commons/Larry D. Moore

SANTIKOS THEATRES MAYAN PALACE 14   Inner South Side
1918 SW Military Drive
San Antonio, TX 78221
210-923-5531; **santikos.com**

> **PEOPLE HAVE REPORTED** hearing the sound of chains being dragged along the floor and banging on the ceiling, especially when they are alone at this theater.

STINSON MUNICIPAL AIRPORT   Inner South Side
8535 Mission Road, #200
San Antonio, TX 78214
210-207-1800; **sanantonio.gov/ssf.aspx**

> **ORIGINALLY ESTABLISHED** in 1915 as Stinson Field and located about 7 miles south of downtown San Antonio, Stinson Municipal Airport is the second oldest general aviation airport in continuous operation in the United States. It was used by the U.S. Army Air Forces as a training facility during World War II and afterward returned to the city of San Antonio for civil

use. Its features include a renovated historic main terminal, the Texas Air Museum, and an adjacent haunted cemetery. Witnesses have reported seeing blue lights over certain graves at night. Some claim to have seen these lights from nearby Mission Road when driving past, and one of the older hangers is reputed to be haunted by the ghost of a man who was killed while starting his aircraft.

LAMBERMONT   Midtown San Antonio
950 E. Grayson St.
San Antonio, TX 78208
210-271-9145; **www.lambermontevents.com**

INSPIRED BY CASTLES he saw while serving as U.S. ambassador to Belgium, statesman and lawyer Edwin Holland Terrell commissioned noted Texas architect Alfred Giles to design this imposing structure and had it built in 1894. He named his chateau Lambermont, after a foreign business associate, and lived in it with his family until his death in 1910. It has had a succession of owners since then and for several years was operated as Terrell Castle Bed and Breakfast until becoming Lambermont Events and used as a wedding venue and for overnight accommodations. The historic home is reputed to be haunted by the original lady of the house, who has reportedly been seen in the library in particular, and by a number of children, whom people sometimes claim to see or hear playing on the stairs.

TRINITY UNIVERSITY   Midtown San Antonio
One Trinity Place
San Antonio, TX 78212-7200
800-trinity; **trinity.edu**

TRINITY UNIVERSITY is a private liberal arts college founded in 1869 with a campus located in the Monte Vista Historic District, adjacent to Brackenridge Park. It has a number of significant and historical buildings, some of which are reputed to be haunted. One of these is the Chapman Center, where, on the lower level in particular, people, including campus police officers and janitorial staff, have suddenly begun to feel uncomfortable and that they needed to leave quickly. Another is the William Knox Holt Center, which many housekeeping staff members will not enter alone or at night.

GREATER SAN ANTONIO

Wikimedia Commons/Billy Hathorn

AUMONT HOTEL   Guadalupe County

301 N. Austin St.
Seguin, TX 78155
830-372-4747

DESIGNED BY PROMINENT TEXAS architect Atlee B. Ayers, who later planned courthouses for Refugio, Cameron, Jim Wells, and Kleburg counties, the elegant Aumont Hotel opened in 1916. The historic building has been thoroughly renovated but is no longer a hotel and now rents out office space and apartments. Numerous accounts of paranormal activity have been noted over the years, and there is reason to believe that some of the Aumont Hotel's guests may have never checked out.

BEXAR-BULVERDE AREA VOLUNTEER FIRE DEPARTMENT
Comal County

Station #104
23103 Bulverde Road
San Antonio, TX 78259
830-980-4733; **bexarbulverdevfd.org**

NUMEROUS PEOPLE have had inexplicable experiences at the Bulverde Area Volunteer Fire Department (in Bulverde a short distance from City Hall) that they have attributed to ghosts. Incidents personnel at the station have reported include walking into rooms and seeing chairs spinning; finding a casserole pan that was at the bottom of a sink, underneath dishes, broken on the floor by itself; hearing a disembodied voice yelling in German; noticing blades falling off of ceiling fans; and feeling an unseen presence touch them. While the station is relatively new, there is no telling what might have once been on or near it—and there is a small, private, 19th-century graveyard located just 200 yards behind it, which some people have linked to the weird events.

CAVE WITHOUT A NAME   Kendall County
325 Kreutzberg Road
Boerne, TX 78006
830-537-4212; **cavewithoutaname.com**

CAVE WITHOUT A NAME is a beautiful, natural, living cavern that has six major chambers filled with magnificent formations of stalactites, stalagmites, delicate soda straws, cave drapery, flowstones, rimstone dams, and more. It also has a tumultuous history that includes being used by bootleggers during Prohibition and the drowning death of someone working at the cave when heavy rains caused water in it to rise suddenly. A number of paranormal investigators have recorded anomalies of various sorts in the cavern and have reason to think it might be haunted by spirits from a number of different eras.

DIENGER BUILDING   Kendall County
106 E. Blanco Road
Boerne, TX 78006
830-249-8240; **diengercenter.org**

IN 1882, Joseph Dienger, the son of German immigrants, purchased a plot of land on the main plaza in the town of Boerne and two years later began construction on a large limestone dry-goods store. Dienger continued to ex-

pand this struc-
ture, adding a
second story to
serve as a home
for him, his wife,
and their seven
children, and his
business thrived
as Boerne grew
and developed
into a health spa.
An aging Dienger
sold the building
a few years be-
fore he died in 1950, and it subsequently served as a grocery store, boarding
house, feed store, private home, restaurant, private club, tavern, offices,
and public library.

Paranormal phenomena of all sorts have been reported since at least
the late 1960s, when the Antlers Restaurant opened in the building. Many
believe it to be haunted by the ghost of Dienger, which has manifested to
express his dislike of drinking.

"His spirit soon began to demonstrate this apparent disapproval by
slamming doors, rattling windows, and turning lights on and off in the old cellar," Docia Schultz Williams says in her classic *Spirits of San Antonio and
South Texas*. "Once, Mrs. Dienger apparently helped in the protest, because
the silhouette of a woman crossing the Trophy Room was seen. Incredibly, it
just passed through a solid wall!" The proprietors of the restaurant responded
to this supernatural activity by maintaining a table for the Diengers, a custom
continued by subsequent owners that seemed to placate the spirits and led
some to feel they were a protective presence.

Other paranormal activity people have reported over the years includes
objects being moved, hurled, and sometimes relocated from one part of the
building to another; doors locking or unlocking on their own; people being
touched by unseen presences; disembodied footsteps; sounds of laughter
and conversation in unoccupied areas; spectral voices speaking on an inter-
com; and the appearance of apparitions, including one believed to be Dienger.

As of this writing, the Dienger Building is closed to the public but owned by a nonprofit association that is converting it into "a cultural and heritage center" that may allow for some opportunities for paranormal investigation.

GUADALUPE RIVER STATE PARK   Comal County, Kendall County
3350 Park Road 31
Spring Branch, TX 78070
830-438-2656; **tpwd.state.tx.us/state-parks/guadalupe-river**

GUADALUPE RIVER STATE PARK was opened to the public in 1983. It comprises a 1,938-acre segment of Texas Hill Country noted for its ruggedness and scenic beauty and has 4 miles of river frontage. Visitors can enjoy a variety of outdoor activities, including birdwatching, camping, canoeing, fishing, hiking, nature study, picnicking, swimming, and tubing, and a 5.3-mile equestrian trail that is also open to mountain biking. People have also noted evidence of paranormal activity at the site, including capturing anomalies in their photographs, and the park has hosted Halloween events that include the telling of ghost stories.

Wikimedia Commons/25or6to4

HUEBNER-ONION HOMESTEAD   Leon Valley/Bexar County
6628 State Highway 16
Leon Valley, TX 78268; **e2sq.com/lvhs/homestead.htm**

THE HUEBNER-ONION HOMESTEAD is a two-story limestone structure that was built in 1862 by immigrant Austrian jeweler and blacksmith Joseph Huebner, who lived in it with his family and operated it as a stagecoach stop. Huebner added the second floor to the house in 1882 and that same year died by bizarre misfortune, poisoning himself when, according to a popular local legend, he mistook kerosene for whiskey.

Judge John F. Onion Sr. and his family moved into the house in 1930 and soon after began to experience strange things and to determine before long that the place was haunted. John F. Onion Jr., the judge's son, recorded the strange things he experienced while living in the house:

You would hear a click, like somebody had stepped on the bottom step of the staircase or stairwell. And then it would automatically come up. It wouldn't be a click here and then a click over here, a click by—it was kind of like somebody was trying to slip up the stairs, you know. And many a time I—when I was sick in bed, I had my eyes glued on the door to see who might walk in. And I never told anybody because I didn't want anybody [to] think I was superstitious or heard ghosts or anything. Then I found out that a good many of the other members of the family had had the same experience.

And I remember my mother had an iron that was an iron you sat down at. It wasn't a hand iron; it was a big machine iron that you could roll something. And then you had a little click on the side—you pushed your leg against it—and the iron would come down, and you'd roll this big roller under the iron and iron something. You push the click, and the iron would raise up, and then you could readjust it. Well, it made such a distinctive noise.

And I always remembered one morning—I guess I was 13 or 14—my dad was going to work. And when he left, car tires on the gravel woke me up, and we were sleeping out on the upstairs porch because we didn't have air-conditioning in those days. . . . and that machine was in one of the inner bedrooms, and I heard it running. And I heard the click. Heard the iron come down; I heard the click. And I thought, well, my mother was ironing something. So I lay there, and my brother was in a different bed; he was sound asleep. And so finally I got up, went into my bedroom off the porch, dressed, and went down to the kitchen. And when I opened the door to the kitchen, my mother turned around and said, "What were you ironing upstairs?" I said, "I wasn't ironing. You were." She says, "No, I've been down here in the kitchen since your—before your dad left even." It was so vivid to both of us at different locations. We both went together back up to where the iron was, and it was just as cold as it could be. My brother was still asleep on the porch. So I said, "I'll never explain that one."

Today the Huebner-Onion Homestead is located in Leon Valley, an independent city completely surrounded by San Antonio, and is being maintained, restored, and turned into a museum and learning center by the local historical commission. Features of the site beyond the home include nature trails, Joseph Huebner's gravesite, and a Texas Historical Marker. It continues to maintain a reputation for being haunted.

OAR HAUS   Comal County
384 Waterway Pass
New Braunfels, TX 78130
830-542-9085; **vrbo.com/506241**

THE OAR HAUS is a vacation-rental cabin located on a private 3-acre park-like section of the Guadalupe River between New Braunfels and Seguin. Most people go there for the beautiful scenery and recreational opportunities, but ghosthunters will likely find some things to interest them as well, including the nearby family cemetery of the owners.

"Our nephew and I were taking pictures when we both saw something in the trees," Nicole Bailey, who spent Easter weekend 2014 there, told me. "I snapped pictures while this shape dashed back and forth through the trees. It ended up right on the tree as if it were trying to hide, and then dashed away. The camera picked it up as an orangeish glow . . . . It was definitely a unique experience and left us speechless for a moment. The place felt very spiritually active to us."

Wikimedia Commons/Billy Hathorn

PALACE THEATRE   Guadalupe County
314 S. Austin St.
Seguin, TX 78155
830-379-2428; **cinematreasures.org/theaters/4206**

BUILT IN THE LATE 1940s, the historical Art Deco–style Palace Theatre now hosts a variety of events and programs for the general public and has two screens available for these purposes. Its larger theater has 350 seats with a 40-foot silver movie screen and a stage; its smaller theater on the second floor has 160 seats, and a concession stand and bar complement the lobby area. Co-located with the theater is the Seguin Cine Museum, a collection of old motion-picture films, cameras, editing equipment, and related memorabilia that covers the history of entertainment media from 180 A.D. to the present. The museum is open during events that take place at the Palace Theatre but also can be viewed on an appointment basis during off times.

Over the years, people have experienced all sorts of paranormal phenomena in the theater. In 2012, for example, a paranormal group conducting an investigation saw plugs pull themselves out of outlets, had electronic equipment destroyed, had scratches appear on the backs of two of its members, and recorded EVPs.

Texas Lutheran University   Guadalupe County
1000 W. Court St.
Seguin, TX 78155
830-372-8000; **tlu.edu**

FOUNDED IN 1891, Texas Lutheran University is situated on a 184-acre campus about 35 miles east of San Antonio in Guadalupe County. Like many historic institutions of this sort, it has many old buildings and no shortage of ghost stories and reputed paranormal activity. One of these is the Wupperman Little Theatre, where a trap door on the stage opens by itself, lights turn on and off on their own, and people claim to see the ghost of a little girl in a blue dress who appears to want to play hide-and-seek. Another is the Trinity Hall dormitory, where people report seeing blinds fluttering and lights flickering off and on even when no one is inside it.

Woman Hollering Creek   Bexar, Comal, and Guadalupe Counties
13850 Interstate 10 Frontage Road
Converse, TX 78109
(29.493151, −98.207693)

ONE OF THE MORE TERRIFYING ghost legends of south Texas is that of *La Llorona*, which tells of a "weeping woman" whose child has drowned in a stream or river and who wanders its banks looking for it. She is a malignant and dangerous spirit who preys upon the living and attempts to drag into the water those unfortunate enough to encounter her. "La Llorona is most often described as a young mother, distraught over the loss of her lover and father to her children. In a fit of rage and sadness, she murders her young children and disposes of their bodies in the river before taking her own life," ghosthunter April Slaughter writes. "It is often said that her unfortunate soul was denied entrance into heaven for the gruesome act and her soul is destined to wander the earth forever."

One of the places people claim to see *La Llorona* drifting among the trees and clad in a flowing white gown is Woman Hollering Creek, which flows east of San Antonio and takes its name from the presumed presence of the specter. This often-dry seasonal stream intersects with Interstate 10 near the town of Converse. (The location coordinates given above are one spot where people can access it.)

A number of other local legends and their locations are quite possibly variations of the *La Llorona* legend or interpretations of its manifestations, including that of the San Marcos River Entity, an invisible presence people have reported around the nearby town of Luling.

AUSTIN

AUSTIN'S INN AT PEARL STREET   Downtown Austin
809 W. Martin Luther King Jr. Blvd.
Austin, TX 78701; **innpearl.com**

THIS BOUTIQUE HOTEL is located on Judge's Hill in one of downtown Austin's historic neighborhoods. First official record of the building can be found in the Austin City Directory of 1914, when it was the private residence of prominent 26th Judicial District Judge Charles A. Wilcox, his wife, Stella, and their five children. Reports from people claiming to have seen the ghost of Stella Snider carrying and comforting a sick child are among the paranormal phenomena associated with this site. Other incidents include accounts of lights coming on even when power to the building is shut off.

CLAY PIT   Downtown Austin
1601 Guadalupe St.
Austin, TX 78701
512-322-5131; **claypit.com**

IN 1872, merchant Rudolph Bertram bought the building that currently houses the Clay Pit Indian restaurant and lived there for eight years before converting the lower level into a grocery, general store, and saloon and moving his family to the upper floor. Visitors and staff of the establishment and the one that preceded it, Bertram's Restaurant, report hearing sounds of revelry upstairs that disappear when investigated. People also claim to see the ghost of a young child, possibly the spirit of Bertram's son, who died of typhoid fever when the family was residing in the building. Local legends also hold that there was once a tunnel in the basement of this building that led to an adjacent brothel, but it is unclear if it still exists.

BUFFALO BILLIARDS   Downtown Austin
201 E. Sixth St.
Austin, TX 78701
512-479-7665; **buffalobilliards.com/austin**

LOCATED IN AUSTIN'S historic Sixth Street district across from the Driskill Hotel, Buffalo Billiards occupies a building that was built in 1861 by the Ziller family and dubbed the Missouri House. It was touted as Austin's first boarding house and rumored to be a brothel. Paranormal events include people being touched by unseen hands and the specter of a man in 19th-century attire who walks through walls where doors used to be located.

CARRINGTON HOUSE   West Campus Austin

1900 David St.
Austin, TX 78705
512-479-0638

BUILT IN 1877, this English country-style house was part of an original homestead of the Republic of Texas and is located in the West Campus neighborhood adjacent to the University of Texas. It is currently operated as a vacation home and is located on an acre of land, complete with a manicured lawn, shade trees, and a large porch that all give it a country atmosphere despite being in the middle of a large city. Paranormal activity reported at the Carrington House includes typical phenomena like televisions turning on and off by themselves—and less typical events like one man's claim that a ghost shampooed his hair!

DAVID GRIMES PHOTOGRAPHY STUDIO   Downtown Austin

503 Neches St.
Austin, TX 78701
512-659-2133; **davidgrimes.com**

THIS BUILDING that now houses the David Grimes Photography Studio is located in what is reputed to have once been a mortuary whose owner was murdered. It is believed to be haunted, and people have claimed to see on numerous occasions the apparition of a woman.

EANES-MARSHALL RANCH   West Lake Hills/Travis County
903 S. Capitol of Texas Highway (Loop 360)
West Lake Hills, TX 78746

"ALEXANDER EANES (1806–1888) moved to Texas from Mississippi in 1845 and acquired this ranch by 1857," a Texas Historical Marker erected at this location in 1986 reads. "In 1873 he sold the property to his brother, Robert Eanes (1805–1895), who had moved to the area following the Civil War. A log cabin built on the Eanes ranch was the first Eanes School, and the community also assumed the Eanes name. Robert Eanes sold the ranch to his son-in-law, Hudson Boatner Marshall (1862–1951) in 1883. Marshall dismantled the ranch house and moved it to a site adjacent to the nearby creek."

The area once occupied by what became known as the Eanes-Marshall Ranch now lies within the city of West Lake Hills, a small community founded in 1953 that is situated just outside of Austin on the south bank of the Colorado River. It was once occupied by Tonkawa and Comanche Indians and considered to be a wild and dangerous place well into the 1800s. The original Eanes-Marshall ranch house, a wagon barn, and a few other 19th-century buildings were relocated to nearby Eanes Elementary School. The original home of the Roys, another early pioneer family, still stands in the local Addie Roy subdivision. Residents of the area have included musician Willie Nelson and politician Ann Richards.

"At the turn of the century, 'cedar choppers' moved to Westlake Hills to harvest cedar building materials for the ever-burgeoning Austin metropolitan area," a story on the REATX Realty Blog says. "The Eanes' 'old rock school house,' built in 1937, employed teachers who frequently complained—even to the point of carrying pistols—of the rowdy cedar-chopper children forced to attend school with the original Eanes' area descendants."

According to local legend, this area is haunted by a pair of spectral horses that pull a driverless wagon, as well as at least seven individual ghosts. Psychically sensitive people who have tried to contact one or more of them have supposedly passed out as a result.

FADO IRISH PUB   Downtown Austin
214 W. Fourth St.
Austin, TX 78701
512-457-0172; **fadoirishpub.com/austin**

FADO IS ONE OF A CHAIN of traditional Irish pubs that was established in the historic warehouse district of Austin in 1997. It is in a building that was reportedly formerly occupied by the Capital City Playhouse before it went out of business. People have reported paranormal activity that suggests that the spirits of some of the former actors might still be present.

GARRISON DISTRICT PARK   Southwest Austin
6001 Manchaca Road
Austin, TX 78745; **austinparks.org/our-parks.html?parkid=251**

"THIS WONDERFULLY SHADED PARK offers a jogging trail along with plenty of sand and grass for running," the municipal web page dedicated to it says. "The Garrison pool is a favorite spot for families, perfect for cooling down after an afternoon of play." It is also adjacent to as many as three old burial grounds. Some people claim that while driving along the road that goes around the park they have seen ghostly figures placing flowers on grave plots.

HIDEOUT   Downtown Austin
617 Congress Ave.
Austin, TX 78701
512-443-3688; **hideouttheatre.com**

THE HIDEOUT is an improvisational theatre that makes up most of its performances on the spot and is co-located with the Hideout Coffee House, Austin's oldest independent establishment of this sort. Numerous paranormal events have been reported here over the years, including locked gates opening and faucets turning on and off by themselves.

JACOB'S HILL   Travis and/or Williamson Counties
Wells Branch Parkway
Pflugerville, TX 78705

A CHARACTERISTICALLY VAGUE local legend involves a bridge on one of the roads that intersects with the 3-mile-long stretch of Wells Branch Parkway that lies east of IH-35 and runs through the historic town of Pflugerville, about 14 miles northeast of downtown Austin. According to some of those who have visited the site, if visitors turn off their vehicles and put them in neutral, they will roll across the bridge. Some explanations are similar to those associated with other "gravity hills," where the laws of nature are apparently suspended, while others claim that vehicles are instead pushed by the ghosts of two children who were killed by their father and are trying to save others from his wrathful spirit.

LITTLEFIELD BUILDING   Downtown Austin
106 E. Sixth St.
Austin, TX 78701

> **IN 1910,** banker and entrepreneur George Littlefield erected an office build-
> ing to house his American National Bank, which was then located in the ad-
> jacent Driskill Hotel. The Littlefield Building became the financial center of
> Austin and was the height of opulence when it opened. Its nine stories briefly
> gave it the distinction of being the tallest skyscraper between New Orleans
> and San Francisco. Paranormal activity reported here includes elevators mov-
> ing from floor to floor on their own in the middle of the night, doors closing on
> their own, whispered conversations on unoccupied floors, and figures moving
> in the windows of empty rooms.

LITTLEFIELD HOUSE   Downtown Austin
Corner of Whitis Avenue and West 24th Street
Austin, TX 78705; **utexas.edu**

> **THE LITTLEFIELD HOUSE** is a historic Victorian home on the campus of
> the University of Texas at Austin (UT) that was built in 1893 for Civil War vet-
> eran George Littlefield, a successful cattleman and banker who was a major
> benefactor of the university. When Littlefield's wife, Alice, died in 1935, she
> left the home to UT. Today
> the ground floor is used
> for university functions
> and the upstairs for office
> space by the Office of the
> President.
>
> "Ghost tales about the
> home abound, and their vari-
> ety is exceeded only by their
> vagueness," a story from
> 2002 on the UT website
> says. "One common strain
> in most of the stories is Alice
> Littlefield, Major Littlefield's
> wife. Some say that Major
> Littlefield locked Alice up in
> the attic when he was away
> so she would not be grabbed

Wikimedia Commons/John Cummings

by Yankees who might be strolling by and oblivious to the fact that the Civil War was over. According to lore, while languishing in the attic she was assaulted by bats, and her shrieks of terror reverberate in the mansion to this day. Others say that the ghost of Alice can still be heard banging out a chord or two on the old piano on the first floor. Some accounts paint Alice as a melancholic, depressive, agoraphobic woman who slowly and quietly went insane later in life. Others stress her deep concern for her husband's welfare and her fears for his safety when he was away. Her ghost is said to restlessly roam the attic, peering out the windows, watching for his return."

Staff working in the Littlefield House also have described foreboding presences, strange smells, and items being moved around when no one was in the building.

MUGSHOTS   Downtown Austin
407 E. Seventh St.
Austin, TX 78701
512-236-0008; **mugshotsaustin.com**

"THE BUILDING IS BELIEVED to have been originally constructed in 1872 by Mr. Jeremiah Sheehan, who worked as a contractor and owned a limestone quarry where the Austin Women's Club exists today," the website for this "best dive bar" says. "Col. B. A. Risher owned the building, which was originally constructed as a house, and it soon became the offices and boarding house for the New Orleans stagecoach, which he operated at Sixth and Neches. In 1886 a widow, Fannie Davis, purchased the building and opened a brothel. From 1950 to 1964 the building was known as the Californian Hotel and was a popular place for traveling musicians to stay. Through the years a few people have seen 'The Lady in the Blue Dress' and because of that, we've been featured in a few books and on the Austin Ghost Tour."

Paranormal phenomena experienced here include seeing the ghost of Fannie Davis in a beautiful blue dress and hearing a particular piece of music, reportedly an oboe concerto, played again and again.

NEILL-COCHRAN HOUSE MUSEUM   West Campus Austin
2310 San Gabriel St.
Austin, TX 78705
512-478-2335; **nchmuseum.org**

BUILT IN 1855 as a suburban estate, this impressive Greek Revival house is considered to be one of Austin's three most important historic residences and

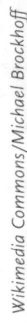

has survived war, neglect, and the immense growth of the University of Texas area and the capital city. Builder Abner Cooke never lived in the home he built for his family. It was instead first used by the Texas Asylum for the Blind, and then, during the tumultuous era of Reconstruction, was occupied by Federal troops. Thereafter it was owned first by Colonel Andrew Neill and his wife, Jennie, and then by the Cochran family, which held it until 1958, when it was acquired by its current owners, the National Society of the Colonial Dames of America in the State of Texas.

Perhaps not surprising considering its age and colorful history, many ghost stories and paranormal phenomena have long been associated with this site. Things reported include hearing disembodied footsteps at night and seeing the specter of Colonel Neill riding his horse around the mansion.

OMNI AUSTIN HOTEL DOWNTOWN   Downtown Austin

700 San Jacinto at Eighth Street
Austin, TX 78701
512-476-3700; **omnihotels.com/FindAHotel/austindowntown.aspx**

THIS BEAUTIFUL LUXURY HOTEL is reportedly the site of numerous suicides by people who have jumped to their deaths. Housekeeping staff have reportedly heard the ghost of one such person, who has been dubbed "Jack," roaming around in the room he occupied before his death.

PARAMOUNT THEATRE   Downtown Austin

713 Congress Ave.
Austin, TX 78701
512-472-5470; **austintheatre.org**

ON OCTOBER 11, 1915, the Paramount Theatre, then called the Majestic Theatre, opened its doors to the public and was home to vaudeville, silent movies, music, dance, and plays for more than 90 years. It is the subject of numerous accounts of paranormal activity, and people working there have reported numerous episodes of strange lights, props moving on their own, and being touched by unseen hands. One person even described a disturbing experience with what he described as a "hag" in the projection room.

Star of Texas Inn   West Campus Austin
611 W. 22nd St.
Austin, TX 78705
866-472-6700; **staroftexasinn.com**

THIS BED-AND-BREAKFAST, located in a historic mansion in downtown Austin, has reportedly been the site of numerous episodes of paranormal activity.

Tavern Restaurant   Downtown Austin
922 W. 12th St.
Austin, TX 78703
512-320-8377; **tavernaustin.com**

WHAT IS NOW KNOWN as the Tavern restaurant was established in 1933 in a building constructed 17 years earlier that was intended to look like a German guesthouse and was used initially as a grocery store.

"Few other Austin gathering places have been home to so many students, soldiers, legislators, presidents, and our town's general citizenry as the Tavern," says the establishment's official history. "Legend has it that a popular yet secretive speakeasy and brothel operated in the second story of the building and that a former employee still haunts the second floor!"

According to one local legend, the Tavern is haunted by the ghosts of a former prostitute named Emily and her daughter, both of whom were reportedly caught in the middle of a fight between two men and killed in the course of it.

Texas Governor's Mansion
Downtown Austin
1010 Colorado St.
Austin, TX 78701
512-463-0063; **txfgm.org**

SINCE 1856, the historic Governor's Mansion has been the home of every governor of Texas and is the oldest continuously inhabited house in the state and fourth-oldest governor's mansion in the United States that has been continuously occupied by a chief executive. The 25-room, 8,920-square-foot

Historic American Buildings Survey/Emil Niggli

Greek Revival–style building is surrounded by trees and gardens and occupies the center of a city block. In 1962 it became the first designated Texas Historic Landmark, was listed in the National Register of Historic Places in 1970, and was declared a U.S. National Historic Landmark in 1974.

On June 8, 2008, while midway through a major renovation, the mansion was badly damaged by a four-alarm fire that an arsonist started with a Molotov cocktail; then-Governor Rick Perry and his wife were not in the house when the attack occurred. On February 2, 2011, a representative of the Texas Rangers announced that an Austin-based anarchist group had been linked to the attack, but no evidence has been offered to support this nor any arrests made.

A number of ghosts are believed to haunt the mansion and have been reported over the years by occupants and visitors alike, along with paranormal phenomena like disembodied footsteps, inexplicable cold spots, the sound of moaning, and doorknobs turning on their own. One of the spirits most often reported is that of Sam Houston, former president and governor of Texas and a hero of its war of independence, particularly in his bedroom and the area where he once hung his hat. Another specter people claim to have seen is that of a young man, ostensibly the 19-year-old nephew of Governor Pendleton Murrah, who killed himself with a pistol in 1864 after having his proposal of marriage refused.

ZACH (ZACHARY SCOTT) THEATRE   South Austin

202 S. Lamar St.
Austin, TX 78704
512-476-0541; **zachtheatre.org**

FOUNDED IN 1933 as Austin Civic Theatre, ZACH Theatre is the oldest continuously operating stage in Texas and one of just 10 original resident acting companies in America. It was renamed Zachary Scott Theatre Center in 1968 in honor of Austin-raised, Academy Award–nominated film star Zachary Scott. Various sorts of paranormal phenomena have been reported at the theater over the years, including evidence of ghosts that steal or swap out performer's possessions, move prop lights, and haunt the aisles.

TEXAS HILL COUNTRY

FORT MARTIN SCOTT   Fredericksburg/Gillespie County

1606 E. Main St.
Fredericksburg, TX 78624
830-997-7521; **ftmartinscott.org**

FORT MARTIN SCOTT was established on December 5, 1848, and was the first U.S. Army post on the western frontier of Texas to protect settlers and travelers from Indian depredations. Its site was also likely used by Texas Rangers as they patrolled in and around what is now Gillespie County during the 1830s and 1840s. Texas Ranger Colonel John H. Moore, with three companies of volunteers, pursued native warriors throughout the area in 1839–1844, and during this era Captain John Coffee Hays and his Ranger company were reportedly involved in actions at Enchanted Rock and other nearby locations. The fort was closed in 1853 but was thereafter periodically used as a camp by the U.S. 2nd Cavalry under Robert E. Lee, Texas Rangers, and the Confederate States Army. Then, in September 1866, General Philip H. Sheridan and the U.S. 4th Cavalry used the fort to secure the frontier once again from possible Indian depredations. It was finally abandoned altogether and then sold to and occupied by the Braeutigan family until being purchased by the city of Fredericksburg in 1959.

Ghostly lore associated with the fort, which has been partially reconstructed, includes reports of spectral soldiers, Rangers, and Indians. The spirit of John T. Braeutigan, who turned the stone guardhouse into a tavern and dance hall and is reported to have been robbed and murdered there in 1884, may be among those who haunt the site.

Kerr County Courthouse

Kerrville/Kerr County
700 Main St.
Kerrville, TX 78028
830-792-2200; **co.kerr.tx.us**

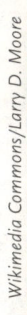
Wikimedia Commons/Larry D. Moore

KERRVILLE WAS SETTLED by people of European descent in the 1840s on ground that archeological evidence shows has been occupied for some 10,000 years. According to one local legend, the grounds of the Kerr County Courthouse are haunted by the ghosts of an unhappy couple, one of a woman who was murdered, and the other of her boyfriend, who reportedly hanged himself after killing her.

LOVER'S LEAP   Junction/Kimble County

County Road 182
Junction, TX 76849
(30.477466, –99.759232)

> **THIS PUBLICLY ACCESSIBLE OVERLOOK** outside the town of Junction provides striking views of the surrounding terrain. A number of variant ghost legends are associated with this site. In one, an Indian maiden, despairing that her lover never returned from a raid, flings herself from the cliff and into the ravine below. In another, a young Indian couple forbidden to marry one another climb to the top of the cliff where they had often met and leaped to their deaths. In all variations of the tale, the unquiet spirits of those who died for love at this spot continue to haunt it into the afterlife.

SCHREINER UNIVERSITY   Kerrville/Kerr County

2100 Memorial Blvd.
Kerrville, TX 78028-5697
800-343-4919; **schreiner.edu**

Wikimedia Commons/Billy Hathorn

SCHREINER UNIVERSITY WAS FOUNDED in 1923 by the Presbyterian Church on land along the Guadalupe River donated by Hill Country rancher, merchant, and former Texas Ranger Captain Charles Schreiner. It was intended as a place "for high-grade instruction and military training to boys and young men as preparation for college and university work." Delaney Hall, one of the buildings on campus, is reportedly haunted by at least eight ghosts, two of which are believed to be those of former students.

"We just finished working on a remodel of this building," a workman named Donald posted to the Haunted Places website in February 2014. "Tools would disappear and we would find them in another room later. Materials would disappear and we would find them on a different floor or room a week later. Nothing stayed where you put it down." Other people claim to have seen shadowy figures moving around in the windows of the building when it is closed up.

WIMBERLEY   Hays County
28 miles southwest of Austin and 46 miles northeast of San Antonio
(29.995555, −98.100833); **cityofwimberley.com**

WIMBERLEY STARTED AS A TRADING POST near Cypress Creek in 1848, the year Hays County was organized, and had various names over the years. William Carvin Winters built a gristmill at the site in 1856 and it was subsequently sold to the Cude family in 1864 and to Pleasant Wimberley in 1874. Over the years, the mill was expanded to process lumber, shingles, flour,

molasses, and cotton. In 1880, Alfred von Stein, a postmaster from San Marcos, applied to have a post office established in the community and dubbed it Wimberleyville, but when his application was granted, the name was shortened to Wimberley. The mill was shut down in 1925, but the community has continued to grow in more recent times into a resort town and destination for tourists and ghosthunters alike. Virtually every historic building in the town is reputed to be haunted and late author Bert Wall wrote numerous books specifically about the ghosts and legends of Wimberley and the surrounding area.

Y.O. Ranch Hotel & Conference Center   Kerrville/Kerr County
2033 Sidney Baker
Kerrville, TX 78028
830-257-4440; **yoranchhotel.com**

NAMED FOR THE NEARBY Y.O. RANCH, this sprawling hotel complex draws upon the history of Texas Hill Country for its theme and is full of antiques and historical artifacts of all sorts. Paranormal phenomena reported at the hotel include seeing the ghosts of cowboys in the courtyard near the swimming pool between 3 and 4 a.m. and a specter who asks staff members for permission to use the restroom.

Bibliography

FOLLOWING IS A LIST OF SOURCES used to one extent or another in the research for *Ghosthunting San Antonio, Austin, and Texas Hill Country*. For the most part, this section does not include websites that are also listed elsewhere in this book, and in many cases they have been used as sources of information as well.

BOOKS

Broome, Fiona. *Ghosts of Austin, Texas: Who They Are and Where to Find Them* (Schiffer Publishing, 2007).

Dobie, J. Frank. *Legends of Texas Volume II: Pirates' Gold and Other Tales* (Pelican Publishing Company, 1975).

Jordan, Terry G. *Texas Graveyards: A Cultural Legacy* (University of Texas Press, 1982).

Kennedy, Ira. *The History of Enchanted Rock* (Xlibris Corporation, 2010).

Syers, Ed. *Ghost Stories of Texas* (Texian Press, 1981).

Swartz, Lauren M., and Swartz, James A. *Haunted History of Old San Antonio* (The History Press, 2013).

Treat, Wesley, Shade, Heather, and Riggs, Rob. *Weird Texas* (Sterling Publishing Co. Inc., 2005).

Wall, Bert M. *The Devil's Backbone: Ghost Stories from the Texas Hill Country* (Eakin Press, 1996).

Wall, Bert M. *Ghosts of Wimberley #4* (Bert M. Wall, 2003).

Wall, Bert M. *The Long Gray Tunnel: A True Story of Crisis, Spirit, and Recovery* (Sunbelt Eakin, 2002).

Wall, Bert M. *Texas Ghosts & Dreams #5* (Bert M. Wall, 2007).

Williams, Docia Schultz, and Byrne, Reneta. *Spirits of San Antonio and South Texas* (Republic of Texas Press/Wordware Publishing Inc., 1993).

Wlodarski, Robert. *Texas Guide to Haunted Restaurants, Taverns, and Inns* (Taylor Trade Publishing, 2001).

WEBSITES

THE ALAMO   thealamo.org

ALAMO HAUNTS   alamohaunts.blogspot.com

AUSTIN POST CARD   austinpostcard.com

BUMP IN THE NIGHT BLOG   bumpinthenightblog.wordpress.com

CITY OF ALAMO HEIGHTS   alamoheightstx.gov

THE COMFORT NEWS   thecomfortnews.com

DEAD EXPLORER   deadexplorer.com

GHOST HUNTERS OF TEXAS   ghosthuntersoftexas.com

TEXAS STATE HISTORICAL ASSOCIATION/
HANDBOOK OF TEXAS ONLINE   tshaonline.org/handbook

HAUNTED PLACES (TEXAS)   hauntedplaces.org/state/Texas

LEGENDS OF AMERICA   legendsofamerica.com

MYSA   mysanantonio.com

OAK HILL GAZETTE   oakhillgazette.com

RIVARD REPORT   therivardreport.com

SAN ANTONIO EXPRESS-NEWS   expressnews.com

SAN ANTONIO CURRENT   sacurrent.com

SAN ANTONIO GHOST HUNTERS   sanantonioghosthunters.org

SAN ANTONIO GHOST HUNTERS YOUTUBE CHANNEL
youtube.com/user/jdel3113

SISTERS OF CHARITY OF THE INCARNATE WORD   amormeus.org

TEXAS HAUNTED HOUSES   hauntedhouses.com/states/tx

VISIT WIMBERLEY   visitwimberley.com

WIKIPEDIA   wikipedia.org

RESOURCES affiliated with this book that ...and paranormal researchers can use to more fully ...ore haunted sites in San Antonio, Austin, and Texas Hill Country and learn more about ghosthunting in general.

Many purportedly haunted sites also have excellent web pages devoted to them and their nonhaunted histories, and we have listed a number of these with the listings for places in the Additional Haunted Sites section. Be sure also to see the bibliography in this book for potentially useful sources of information that do not appear here or in the other sections.

GHOSTHUNTING SAN ANTONIO, AUSTIN, AND TEXAS HILL COUNTRY (Blog)   ghosthunting-san-antonio.blogspot.com

THIS IS THE OFFICIAL DEDICATED BLOG for *Ghosthunting San Antonio, Austin, and Texas Hill Country*. It is a multimedia site that contains supplemental material based on author Michael O. Varhola's personal visits to haunted places throughout the region and beyond, links to shows he has appeared on, addenda and errata to this book, video and audio files, information about signings and other events, and more.

AUTHOR MICHAEL O. VARHOLA (Facebook Page)
facebook.com/MichaelOVarhola

THIS IS MICHAEL O. VARHOLA'S official author page on Facebook and one of the main venues he uses for posting information about the projects he is working on. Follow it to get exclusive information not available anywhere else.

AMERICA'S HAUNTED ROAD TRIP (Website)
americashauntedroadtrip.com

THIS IS THE OFFICIAL WEBSITE of the *America's Haunted Road Trip* series of travel guides to haunted places people can visit. Among other things, it features articles on haunted sites throughout the country.

America's Haunted Road Trip (Facebook Page)
facebook.com/AHRT.books

> This is the official Facebook page for the *America's Haunted Road Trip* series of travel guides and a source for information about this book and others in the line, author events, and more.

Sisters Grimm (Website)
sistersgrimmghosttour.com

> This is the website for Sisters Grimm, a company that runs ghost tours throughout downtown San Antonio most nights and which begins its various events either at that haunted Menger Hotel or adjacent Alamo Plaza.

Articles

"Fence at Alamo Cement Company"
ftp://ftp.thc.state.tx.us/nr_program/Dionicio%20Rodriguez/NR%20
Alamo%20Cement%20Fence.pdf

"On the Job Injury: Man Killed at Alamodome"
sanantonio.legalexaminer.com/workplace-injuries/on-the-job-injury-man
-killed-at-alamodome

"Spooky Politics: Texas Capital Home to Ghosts"
http://usatoday30.usatoday.com/news/nation/2008-10-28
-1127242212_x.htm

"West Lake Hills"
reatx.com/west-lake-hills.php

"Woman Mysteriously Falls Down Elevator Shaft She Heard Voices In and Dies"
reddit.com/r/Thetruthishere/comments/19hshi/woman_mysteriously
_falls_down_elevator_shaft_she

About the Author

MICHAEL O. VARHOLA is a writer who has authored or co-authored 34 books and games—including *Ghosthunting Maryland* and *Ghosthunting Virginia,* the swords-and-sorcery novel *Swords of Kos: Necropolis,* and two fantasy writer's guides—and published more than 120 games and related publications. He is the founder of game company Skirmisher Publishing LLC (**skirmisher.com**), editor-in-chief of *d-Infinity* game magazine (**d-infinity.net**), and editor of the *America's Haunted Road Trip* series of travel guides. He has edited, published, or written for numerous publications, including the *New York Times,* is a combat veteran who served eight years in the U.S. Army, and lives in the Hill Country north of San Antonio, Texas. He also has an active online presence, notably through Facebook, Twitter, and a variety of blogs, forums, and sites.